HOW YOU
SEE IT

HOW YOU
DON'T

HOW YOU
SEE IT

HOW YOU
DON'T

*Discover the Magic & Power
of Your Own BELIEFS*

❖   ❖   ❖

DAVID B. BOLEN, II

Award-Winning Author of
The Essence *of* Living
Reaching Beyond Global Insanity

NEW VERITY

PUBLISHING

Published by New Verity Publishing
726 Keene Drive, Suite 103
Medford, Oregon 97504
For promotional or order information only:
Telephone: (541) 857-0269 or Fax: (541) 857-0274

Edited by Nancy B. Hackleman

Cover Design & Book Production by Chris Rose-Merkle

Author Photos by Christopher Briscoe

Printed in the United States of America by
  Commercial Printing Company Inc.

Library of Congress Catalog Card Number: 96-092044

ISBN: 0-9641909-1-5 Pbk.

ACKNOWLEDGEMENTS

*This book is dedicated to my parents
and my sisters for their years of support
and unconditional love.*

*Thank you for sharing with me
the most important gift of life,
believing that I can be whatever I desire.*

Contents

WE CALL THAT LIFE!

When we fantasize we call that dreaming
When we remember we call that memory
When we are in the moment we call that living
When we forget we call that aging
When we integrate them all, we call that Life!

When we feel close we call that love
When we feel wronged we call that blame
When we feel angry we call that power
When we feel great we call that happy
When we have feelings, we call that Life!

When we imagine the good we call that joy
When we imagine the bad we call that fear
When we imagine the years we call that old
When we imagine the freedom we call that youthful
When we imagine, we call that Life!

When we believe our judgments we call that righteous
When we believe our expectations we call that hope
When we believe our thoughts we call that feeling
When we believe our imagination we call that reality
When we believe our beliefs, we call that Truth!

We call that Life!

❖

PREFACE

You will soon find that where you are is where you always were before you woke up.

Whereas modern psychology has focused on things like our ego, inner child, and dysfunctional families, some psychologists and counselors are discovering that focusing on the pathology of our being can be stifling. Advocates who believe we can make greater strides in our personal growth by emphasizing our health say that concentrating on perceived inadequacies merely keeps the patient attached to thoughts that may not be relevant to creating a more fulfilling life today. For those people who might prefer an alternative approach to creating joy in their lives, becoming the expert on their own lives may be the best solution.

In our search for acceptance, we compare the speed of our emotional and physical recovery to others to determine if we are normal. By accepting such comparisons, we become indoctrinated with the belief that we must endure our pain for as long as is normal. While this may make us feel comfortably normal, we may be undermining our ability to expeditiously establish our emotional well-being.

The biggest advancements in personal growth can come from uncomfortable circumstances, including major changes. Unaware that change occurs when we stay put as well as when we initiate it, we forget to think about what it is we really want. Asking this basic question may be more important than, for example, exploring what happened in our childhood.

Our thoughts often focus more on what we don't want. It is fear that keeps most people focused on avoiding what they don't want: a relationship breakup, job loss, financial ruin, weight gain, sickness, loss of control, victimization, and the list goes on. Many have now realized that this fear-based thinking is precisely what keeps people in therapy, buying self-help books and going to personal growth workshops. While these individuals continue to search for the secrets to lasting happiness, they may be overlooking the fact that what they seek already exists. What most of us don't realize is that the combination of thoughts and beliefs leads to emotions and then to behavior. With this awareness, we may be in the position to create the *essence* of what we want without the assistance of or dependence on others.

So how do you get control of your thoughts? It has been discovered that we can overcome our fear-based thoughts by choosing to think about creating the *essence* of what we want in every moment. The answer sounds so simple that it frightens some skeptics. The reason this may not work for some people is because of their belief that life is complex and that there are no simple answers. Again, by simply implementing another belief system that alters our experiences, we may be able to make dramatic changes in the quality of our lives.

This brings forward the issue of health. Health has been interpreted to mean the absence of ailment. However, the more appropriate view of health may be the ability to heal. Our ailments can often signal the start of the healing process. So next time you are feeling depressed or have a sore throat, you may want to acknowledge that you are getting a message from your healthy spirit that you are in the process of healing, not in further breakdown. Again, this is a question of choosing to believe in your potential. This also means accepting the responsibility to choose a belief that will help you create the life you want. Ultimately, you are accountable for recognizing that life has infinite possibilities that are as close to you as your chosen thought processes and beliefs.

Life has an inherent intelligence and the capacity for adjustments, healing, and the ability to cope with the abnormal. So our natural coping mechanisms can often assist us through those difficult times. Many people lose perspective by thinking about those harmful circumstances that are outside of their control. Why increase stress unnecessarily by worrying excessively about what *could* happen? Too many people become confused in life dealing with the illusionary concept of the *hereafter*. Likewise, there are many people who are immersed in the *herebefore*. In other words, they stay attached to thoughts about what happened several generations ago or even in a past life. By overemphasizing our past or future lives, we deprive ourselves of a joyous experience in our present existence that maintains a healthy mind-body state. Health and healing of the mind-body are tied to our present condition.

We best ensure our emotional success by letting go of the belief that we must fix ourselves and be in a constant state of personal growth. The truth may be that we are already perfect the way we are. An obsession with personal growth is really a distraction from our true potential to create what we want in each moment. If we want peace, we must be peaceful; if we want love, we must be loving; if we want joy, we must be joyous. Unfortunately, some have tried to convince us that to be happy is to be in denial. After all, isn't finding happiness the reason we go to therapy, read self-help books, and go to workshops? The only thing we have denied is the ability to change our thoughts and beliefs to create an emotionally rewarding life. Many enlightened souls now know that there is joy in recognizing the power of our own beliefs.

*The greatest power of all is realized when
the universe within our thoughts and beliefs
connects with the universe we perceive
to be external to ourselves.
It is from this source that we create
true transformation, health, joy,
love, and success.*

INTRODUCTION

I smiled and the world smiled back.

After writing my first book, *The Essence of Living: Reaching Beyond Global Insanity*, I did not intend to write a second book on the same subject matter. However, what I discovered from readers was that many people who embraced the philosophy of my first book still had difficulty creating desired changes in their daily lives. I realized that my first book had accomplished what I had intended, i.e., to be thought provoking. While this helped to open the minds of some people, they still seemed unclear about how they could use this new perspective to their benefit. The book was too abstract for some readers who were only familiar with traditional thought processes and beliefs.

In addition to correspondence from many who found great value from *The Essence of Living*, I also received calls and letters from readers who were not convinced that making changes in their lives was something they wanted to do or could do. Some people who wanted to make changes in their lives and were prepared to confront their fears still could not feel fulfillment in their lives. This phenomenon was puzzling to me at first. After I spent time with people going through a workbook I developed to complement *The Essence of Living*, I started to see a consistent pattern emerge. I now understand why those people were not getting what they ultimately wanted. I identified three primary reasons why people are not effective at creating the life experiences that they want.

First, most people are not accustomed to dedicating time to understand their beliefs and rethink their lives. Instead, they often wait until an external circumstance or condition arises and creates discomfort. They then reflect on their experience and analyze how they might have reacted differently, hoping, of course, that if a similar situation occurs, they will respond in their preferred manner. To their disappointment, they would find that they consistently did not respond in the way that they wanted.

Secondly, in order to respond in a way that is consistent with their *essence*, I noticed that people usually seek assistance from others to find help. Despite the workshops, counseling, and books that they read, they still find only partial evidence of their power to create what they want in life. The common denominator keeping these people from creating the life they want is their beliefs.

After further investigation, I discovered a third reason, which is that most individuals have conflicting beliefs. What this means is that their beliefs about what they want are undermined by an opposing belief that prevents them from manifesting their preferred result in either a physical, emotional, or spiritual form. There was an overwhelming attachment to the physical manifestation of their desires instead of to the emotional or spiritual rewards. Even those who have religious faith sometimes doubt their beliefs about themselves and their ability to create what they want. Without physical proof, most people discard their beliefs and their confidence due to their lack of trust in their own beliefs. The old adage "I'll believe it when I see it" is still very prevalent.

The human brain is programmable. We call the application programs that tell us how to run our lives *beliefs*. As children, our programming is derived from sources external to ourselves. Even as adults, we are most susceptible to external programming from our daily living environment. However, we are also very capable of doing our own self-programming. It is through this ability to program ourselves that we make fundamental changes in our lives.

Any time we break a habit we must undergo a certain degree of self-programming. When we move beyond the realm of reprogramming our behavior, we discover that we can also modify, not only our physical actions, but our emotional state of being as well. With this awareness, we can begin to choose how we emotionally experience life. The emotions that we most prefer to experience in our lives are what I refer to as our *essence*. Our true *purpose* in life is to experience our *essence*.

In Part One of this book, you will begin to understand how the intention of our beliefs is to help us achieve fulfillment, satisfaction, and happiness. You will also discover how conflicting beliefs sabotage even our most noble intentions. One way we can keep a check on these subversive beliefs is by identifying our purpose in life. In Chapter 2, you will have the chance to explore and claim your true purpose in life. If you are armed with a commitment to your purpose, Chapter 3 will reveal basic core beliefs that may not be consistent with your purpose. Of course, one of the biggest obstacles in our lives is fear, which is simply a belief about what might happen. In Chapter 4, you will discover how we can minimize the risk in our lives by examining those beliefs that create fearful thoughts and emotions.

Part Two explores a new paradigm and perspective toward living with success. This new outlook will assist you in viewing your problems as opportunities. Instead of compartmentalizing your life, you will find that life is most rewarding when we balance all the areas in our lives to support our purpose. You will be exposed to the sometimes little used, yet powerful realm of your imagination. You will learn how your imagination can either serve you or downgrade your life experience. The most difficult challenge in life is letting go of our attachments to those things that often bring us discomfort or pain. It is our individual responsibility to exploit the power of our intellect to produce the emotional results we want. Chapter 7 reveals how to integrate your spiritual desires with your physical reality so that you can consistently fulfill your purpose in every moment.

Our intellect produces judgments which are merely subjective assessments that affect how we interpret the world around us. We often use categorization as a method of judging to understand our reality quickly. However, in Chapter 8 you will discover how this method may unconsciously predetermine your future experiences.

Part Three investigates how we can integrate the beliefs that bring us our greatest joy and fulfillment. After our basic survival needs have been met, the three most significant areas of our lives are money, relationships, and health. To fulfill our purpose in all of these areas, we must understand what beliefs work best for us and which ones make our lives difficult. We can avoid numerous problems by becoming experts in our own lives. When we choose to acknowledge our purpose, expertise, and perfection, we hold the key to unlocking our creativity. Our lives transform in ways that others may describe as miraculous or just plain lucky. When we experience what we want unexpectedly, we also consider ourselves lucky. Fortunately, we don't have to depend on luck alone. After reading this book, I trust you will have the awareness to create the *essence* of what you want in your daily life. *Now* is the time to fulfill your purpose and make a difference in your life and in the lives of those around you.

Your beliefs are the magic that makes
every illusion seem real!

❖

Part One

A Look Behind the Curtain

❖ ❖ ❖

Chapter 1

How Beliefs Influence Our Experience

*Discovery is knowing
what you didn't think you knew.*

If we are to truly experience the essence of our heart's desires, we must understand ourselves in the context of our current belief structure. Our human experience is determined by these beliefs. In fact, every religious, political, cultural, ethnic, scientific, or social belief that we adopt is designed to ultimately enhance our experience or condition. The truth is that not all beliefs serve to enrich our lives. Often our beliefs keep us repeating old patterns of behavior with painful results. The challenge, of course, is to discern which beliefs help us feel fulfilled and which beliefs create discomfort in our lives. While there are many approaches, methods, and techniques for improving our lives, it seems that some roads are often long and sometimes expensive detours to our true understanding of how to create the *essence* of what we want.

For most people, the challenge is how to reveal those beliefs that cause the discomfort. This is a surprisingly easy process, but many individuals overlook the obvious. Even professionals in the field sometimes miss opportunities for self-empowerment, perhaps because they themselves do not make this obvious process of evaluating and creating beliefs a part of their own life experience.

We each have the responsibility to choose beliefs that help us get what we want. The only barometer for measuring our success within the beliefs that we choose comes from how we experience life. Unfortunately, many people are focused more on the process of *how* to get what they want than on *what* they want. When we live primarily according to processes, we deny ourselves the chance to simply enjoy the beauty of our intention.

The process of creation is nothing more than a fabrication of our imagination. It is from our imagination that life comes to life either in the form of memories or our projections about the future. Both states of imagination can only exist in the present moment we call *now*. What most of us fail to realize is that no matter what event or circumstance we find ourselves in, our experience is always determined by our imagination about what is happening to us at that moment. If we choose to imagine the situation from fear, we have a different experience than if we imagine it from comfort and delight.

Where Beliefs Come From

Drawing conclusions about what we perceive to be true is called belief.

What I have discovered is that our imagination is one source of our reality. Another source of our reality comes from those beliefs that we have been programmed with when we were in a state of fear. In other words, when we feel our survival is threatened or when we are in severe pain, we are most susceptible to the programming of our beliefs. The most vulnerable time for many of us is when we are children. Many of our lasting beliefs are instilled during our youth. In other instances, we are programmed through fear as adults. We may shift our childhood beliefs as we get older just because we are supposed to or should.

However, throughout life we will continue to change beliefs. Often we are unaware that our beliefs have changed. We are constantly being reprogrammed through the influence of external stimuli such as schools, churches, families, social groups, counselors, friends, work environments, television, movies, books, magazines, newspapers, and music. These types of input reflect and influence our cultural values. We are often unaware that when our beliefs change, our lives might be emotionally enhanced or downgraded. With constant external stimuli and an internal lack of awareness, it is sometimes difficult to determine which beliefs and values work well for us and which ones don't.

Cultural Values

A culture collectively absorbs the individual identity into a patterned group behavior, hence diminishing the uniqueness of both.

There are those who believe we can create what we want by subscribing to a set of behavioral values established within a culture. The logic says, "If I do all the right things, say all the right things, and act a certain way, then I will be well off." Contrary to this logic, those who are pioneers of their souls discover a quality of life and a sense of purpose that far exceeds the results of conformity to social norms. The emphasis is not on developing countercultural attitudes or beliefs but on understanding and fulfilling our individual purpose.

These cultural values and traditions are merely beliefs that are intended to bring order and conformity to a society. When we adhere to such beliefs, we tend to feel secure. However, there are many examples of cultural values or traditions that do not provide security or safety for all citizens. For example, women around the world have been victims of abuse, torture, bondage, slavery, and mutilation, all in the name of tradition and cultural values. We have also seen this type of behavior directed towards different races and religions. For instance, most religious or political battles begin with and are perpetuated by the belief that the opposition deserves less humane treatment. Throughout history, we have seen the mistreatment of many socially unacceptable groups by their own governments.

The concept of family values is prevalent in almost all cultures. But what exactly are family values? In some instances, they mean keeping the family together even at the expense of those who are victims of emotional and physical abuse. Is your purpose to sustain an environment of molestation, violence, and intimidation? Of course not! If your purpose includes living harmoniously with others, then you probably realize that your purpose is inconsistent with an abusive family or cultural tradition. Would you prefer to stay in an abusive relationship or let go of your beliefs about family values and create a harmonious living arrangement with someone else? In effect, cultural or family values and beliefs can sometimes undermine our own well-being. Without exploring our own souls for the *essence* of our heart's desires, we cannot begin to implement beliefs that serve us or others.

Personal Values

If anything changes you, let it be you.

On a personal level, our *essence* is always in alignment with our well-being and that of others. That is why it is very important for us to know our purpose and to commit to that purpose. Beliefs that are derived from our *essence* or purpose will always transcend those established by a group, organization, religion, government, or even our own families. Most atrocities in life happen because people misunderstand their true purpose; instead, they subscribe to ill-fated beliefs about control and power.

I have never met a person who felt fulfilled from abusing him- or herself or someone else. If you believe that control and power will make you happy, then you will be unhappy as long as you also believe you don't have power or control. Even those who abuse others in an attempt to feel more powerful seldom retain the feeling of power. Therefore, they must continue finding victims to support their need for control. Perhaps the secret to achieving power and control is to believe that you already have it. What would it feel like to have power and control? Would you feel secure, free, content, comfortable, and maybe respected? If you already know what it feels like to have power and control, why do you need power and control?

The payoff for our beliefs about how we create happiness is not always happiness. Therefore, we must be aware that not only do our own beliefs sometimes undermine our purpose, but so do some of our social values. The only way to determine which values and beliefs are valid for each of us is to monitor our emotional fulfillment and our health. When we experience the emotions that we don't want, that is our clue that we are living according to a belief or beliefs that are not serving our purpose.

Deceptive Beliefs

Reality is merely a perception which is limited by knowledge or what you believe to be true.

The reason we struggle with understanding our beliefs is because once we implement a belief into our lives, we will always find evidence to support our beliefs. In a sense, we never believe that our beliefs are not serving us well. This is why beliefs become self-fulfilling prophecies. Only when we feel threatened do we find ourselves confronting the possibility of changing our beliefs. In fact, only when the perceived threat of pain or death is great do we usually explore alternative beliefs.

We subscribe to beliefs as if they were insurance policies. Various organizations, institutions, social clubs, and religions all ask us to select their insurance policies or beliefs as a way to avoid what we don't want: pain, suffering, and death. Advertisers have used the insurance policy psychology of fear successfully for many years in order to persuade us to buy their products. Fortunately, it is also possible to examine our beliefs under nonthreatening circumstances.

Personal responsibility is the key to changing beliefs. We are and always will be responsible for what we choose to believe and how those beliefs impact our lives. We are also responsible for determining our purpose in life. We are responsible for determining the obstacles that keep us from fulfilling our purpose, and we are responsible for choosing only those beliefs that support us in fulfilling our purpose. Once we assume responsibility for our lives through our beliefs, we discover that life continues to support the fulfillment of our purpose.

Avoidance Strategies

The mind is sometimes like a tunnel
leading in only one direction.

Avoidance strategies normally come cloaked as beliefs that tell us what we don't want. We can generally tell when we adopt this type of strategy because we make the following statements: "I don't want . . . , I can't . . . , I would prefer not to . . . , I should . . . , I am supposed to . . . , I'd better . . . ." This language tells us we are actually engaging in an avoidance strategy. We do this because we are not focused on what we truly want to create; instead, we identify with the consequences resulting from what we don't want.

We use other language that signals an avoidance strategy: We make statements where the subject describes what we don't want. For example, some people may say, "I want my life to be stress free." The reason they cannot create a stress-free life is because they are focused on stress, which is what they don't want. To imagine what they truly want, they would have to say, "I live a relaxed and calm life." In this second statement, they now describe what they want.

People who struggle with their weight also generally focus on their being overweight rather than on aligning themselves with what it feels like to accept themselves and their bodies. Instead of looking in the mirror and saying, "I am fat," they could choose to align themselves with what they truly want and say, "I feel good about myself." I have seldom met anyone who intentionally and successfully lost weight without focusing on their desire to be thinner or healthier. The subject of our beliefs usually determines how we experience our lives. If we believe we are fat, then, regardless of our weight, that is how we experience life—as a fat person. When we can see ourselves as desirable, then we experience life with appreciation.

A woman who wanted to stop smoking said she had difficulty breaking her habit. She constantly resisted pleas from her family to stop smoking and felt annoyed by their persistence. She, too, wanted to stop, but said it seemed too hard and that she didn't like being told what to do. The reason she wanted to stop smoking was for her health. I asked her, "Who is ultimately responsible for your health?" She admitted that her health was her responsibility. "So when are you going to assume responsibility for your health?" I asked. She immediately realized that for many years she had just focused on cigarettes and her family's reaction to her smoking instead of focusing on her health. She had focused on what she didn't want at the expense of improving her own health.

When we are externally oriented and depend on others or expect material items to bring us happiness, we also avoid being personally responsible and self-reliant. Here are other examples of statements that either focus on what we don't want or that don't allow us to acknowledge that what we want may already exist. The following statements in the left-hand column seldom serve us well:

Externally Oriented	vs.	Self-Reliant
"I want to get out of debt."		"I am creating financial freedom."
"I want to avoid unhealthy relationships."		"I create joy & harmony in my life."
"I want someone who will love me."		"I am a loving & lovable person."
"I want to leave this place."		"I am moving to. . . . ."
"I want a 'real' job."		"I am fulfilling my purpose."
"I want to be rich."		"I add value to others' lives wherever I go."
"I want to be respected."		"I love and respect myself."
"I want to be accepted."		"I love others unconditionally."

Some people might discount these statements as simply a difference in semantics. In fact, by not realizing specifically what we are saying, we often remain focused on what we don't want. As long as we try to avoid what we don't want, we are not creating what we do want; we aren't charging our imagination with visions of what we truly want. Without having this clear vision of what we want, it is almost impossible to enter the feeling state that allows us to become familiar with and to know our success.

This very important factor is often absent when people say affirmations, pray, visualize, or meditate. Many focus so intently on what they think they want in the physical or material world that they do not pay attention to the feelings that they want. **Unless we enter the feeling state that we ultimately want, we will not fulfill our purpose or experience the physical manifestation of our desires.**

The true visionary experiences reality
and not just a vision.

Chapter 2

Discovering Your Purpose in Life

Your soul's desire is to fulfill your purpose.

In my book *The Essence of Living*, I present a matrix that connects our external reality (relationships, environment, and profession) with our internal reality (thoughts, emotions, and health). By following simple guidelines that avoid emphasizing materialism, tangible events, or physical actions, the reader defines the *essence* of what he or she wants. *Essence* is merely a description of your preferred state of being, where you have everything you could possibly want in your life. For example, those who filled out the worksheet indicated their preferred state of being and the associated emotions. The list on the next page represents ways in which some describe their purpose in life. In a sense, the *essence* of what we want in life is to fulfill our purpose. Here is a random sampling of words that some people use to define their *essence* or purpose:

Free • Joyous • Happy • Connected • Alive • Harmonious
Loving • Energetic • Enthusiastic • Flowing • Peaceful
Inspired • Fulfilled • Satisfied • Warm • Comfortable • Relaxed
Calm • Nurturing • Strong • Vital • Clear • Stimulated
Balanced • Flexible • Open • Whole • Complete • Fun
Creative • Artistic • Expressive • Beautiful • Confident
Capable • Spontaneous • Excited • Sharing • Trusting
Inventive • Independent • Contributing • Generous • Enduring
Focused • Alert • Awake • Oneness • Light • Fluid • Cozy
Playful • Vibrant • Aligned • Exhilarated • Invigorated
Refreshed • Appreciative • Interactive • Adventurous • Resilient
Passionate • Delighted • Empowered • Integrated • Effective
Aware • Elated • Tranquil • Soothing • Smooth • Euphoric

After reviewing the above list, you may choose some or all of the above words to describe your own purpose. Perhaps you may want to add your own words to this list. At each moment in our lives we either feel consistent with our purpose or we do not. When we feel we are not in alignment with our purpose, it is most likely because we have a belief that causes us to interpret, understand, and see the world as inconsistent with our purpose or *essence*.

While the thought of discarding a belief may feel threatening to some people, the choice to maintain certain beliefs may cause them to live with fear instead of a sense of freedom, trust, and joy. It seems amazing that we will exert tremendous energy, sometimes arguing or fighting to the death for our right to be miserable, yet very few of us will redirect our energy to focus on our right to be happy. If we decide to live with purpose, we will live and die with joy. What greater purpose can we possibly deserve and have?

When we stay aligned with our purpose, we establish our integrity. When we live with integrity, we are not susceptible to the trials and tribulations that pull many people back into a fear-based belief system. We focus on our purpose at all costs, even if the cost is death. And wouldn't we prefer to die having fulfilled our purpose?

The point of living with purpose is to focus not on death but on the celebration, joy, and beauty of life. Of course, if your belief is that life is difficult, you will not see the opportunity to live with peace and tranquility. You will continue to find evidence to support your belief that life is a struggle. Your beliefs will always prove you correct!

The question then arises, "Is it possible to witness pain, suffering, abuse, and death and still create the life you want?" If you answer this question "no," then you will be right. However, if you answered the question "yes," then you will be right. Life is not about judging what we see and feel as right and wrong. In our own minds, our beliefs are always right. Even though we believe we are right, we don't always feel content, satisfied, or fulfilled. Therefore, the point of a belief is not to prove we are right but to help us fulfill our purpose. If a belief does not fulfill our purpose, then we have the power to select another belief that is more consistent with our purpose or *essence*. Most people will project their fear and ask, "What if . . . ?" or they will say, "How about . . . ?", and lastly, "Yeah, but . . . !" When we focus on our fear we cannot focus on our purpose and vice versa.

The beauty of our human experience is that we each share a common purpose and *essence*. I am convinced this is true from the response I have had to my book *The Essence of Living* and from my own life experience traveling and living around the world. The one thing that creates conflict for most people is their belief about how to fulfill their purpose. Based on the years of sustained human conflict, I can only conclude that many of these beliefs about how to fulfill our purpose are not, in fact, serving to fulfill that purpose.

Once again, we must confront our own beliefs, imagination, and fears to determine if we are being truly fulfilled emotionally and spiritually. The opportunity for love, harmony, peace, and joy resides in the thoughts that each of us hold as beliefs. We are responsible for discarding outdated beliefs that merely perpetuate our fear, insecurity, sadness, depression, grief, guilt, shame, frustration, and anger. Whenever we blame another person or event for our discomfort, we cease to acknowledge our ability to create the *essence* of what we truly want. Those who are strongly invested in their beliefs will find reasons that justify and support their current condition, circumstance, and emotional state, even if they are unhappy.

Bolen's Law of Propulsion

A wish never comes true
without first becoming reality.

Beliefs follow what I call *Bolen's Law of Propulsion*. This simple law states that we are propelled through life in the direction of our beliefs. Whatever we choose to believe determines our life experiences. Some people try to take this law and apply its principles to others. Unfortunately, this law applies uniquely to each individual and his or her own beliefs.

In other words, you can't change your belief about someone else and then expect that they will change. However, you can choose to believe that the person possesses the qualities that you prefer. In this case, you will probably see the person differently—with understanding and clarity but without expectations. As a result of acknowledging the preferred qualities in that person, it is possible that you will relate to them with a new disposition. As your attitude shifts, so will your experience of the person.

Denying factual or physical evidence does not apply to Bolen's Law of Propulsion because we are discussing this law in the context of our beliefs or spirituality. In other words, we cannot immediately alter our physical reality; we can only alter the way we respond to our physical reality. For example, if I am feeling the symptoms of a common cold, I may still choose to believe I am healthy. This belief does not alter the fact that I have a sore throat. But believing that I am healthy may empower my immune system and expedite the healing process. Since I trust in my body's immune system, I feel confident, relaxed, and joyful about my state of being without any expectation about how quickly I should feel physically well. By maintaining my emotional or spiritual wellness, I stay consistent with my purpose.

The idea that we can live without expectations and attachment to physical form seems abstract to some people. This might be because they believe that the physical world is what defines their reality. When we live without expectation, we can focus more effectively on fulfilling our purpose. For instance, my purpose in writing this book was to experience the joy of sharing my awareness and knowledge. In this instant while I am writing this book, I am fulfilling my purpose. The *Bolen Law of Propulsion* comes into effect as I realize other opportunities to share this information and fulfill my purpose through public speaking, workshops, and personal relationships which will perpetuate my joy.

I know my thoughts have power. I can create a believable reality that generates emotions consistent with the purpose of my life. Is it all make-believe or is it real? Are my emotions make-believe or are they real? I feel no stress and no fear. Is it make-believe or is it real? Is my life perfect or is it make-believe? I guess that depends on how I answer these questions.

Your purpose will bring you joy and sustenance.

Chapter 3

Is Your Life Perfect?

Living the Perfect Life

*You will never know what you know until
you know that you know everything.*

How would you answer the question if you were asked, "Is your life perfect?" Would you answer, "There is no such thing as perfect" or "It's almost perfect" or "No, my life is not perfect"? Would you dare answer, "My life is absolutely perfect"? Most people do not believe their lives are perfect. Many people don't even know what perfect means to them.

I am asking you now to think about what *perfect* means to you. If you had a perfect life, what would be included and what would be different than what you have now? If you had more money, a more spacious home, a better relationship, improved health, a better job, would your life be perfect? Interestingly, these are the things that most people want. They strive to achieve their goals and, once successful, they feel their lives are still not perfect. How is this possible?

I have discovered that people who define perfect in purely a material, tangible, or otherwise physical sense believe that if their lives were emotionally or spiritually perfect, they would be bored, unhappy, or would simply die. I have often wondered how someone could be bored or unhappy with an emotionally fulfilling life. What I have noticed is that there is an underlying belief that suggests life only has meaning when it is a struggle. Some people believe the value of living comes from overcoming challenges, trials, and tribulations. With this belief system, they will constantly create life-challenging circumstances, regardless of how much financial wealth they have. This may explain why even in affluent societies there are many people who are not happy. They believe that the purpose of life is to struggle because it is through adversity that they grow and learn.

Perhaps if you are reading this book, you also share the same belief about the need for personal growth. However, consider why people are invested in their struggle for personal growth. What is the *essence* of what they want from their personal growth? The *essence* of what most people want is to feel relaxed, peaceful, free, happy, loving, and constructive. Since this is the *essence* of what we want in life, isn't our essential purpose to experience these feelings? What is your purpose in life? Think about the ultimate emotional reward you get for all the things that you aspire to in your life.

Most people aspire to the emotional rewards of feeling whole as a person and connected with others and nature.

This is why we want the companionship of family, children, friends, community, pets, and nature. Despite the fact that we surround ourselves with other people and things, we don't always receive the emotional payoff we want. We still get frustrated, impatient, angry, and lonely. As these emotions consume our psyche, we act out in ways that are often painful to ourselves and others. Yet our original intention was to get an emotional reward, not punishment.

Beliefs About Your Own Personal Awareness

Masquerade no more, for you are truly beautiful.

There are at least two approaches that help us learn to let go of our attachments and our expectations in life. The most prominent approach is to acknowledge and believe that life is difficult, problem-filled, and full of suffering. No doubt we find and dwell on the evidence to support this belief. One intention of this approach to life is to help us accept our traumatic and painful experiences as normal. If we feel normal, then we hope we will stop trying to fight and resist the inevitable pain of living. The expected outcome is that we will be less resistant and, therefore, less stressed. Ultimately, if we reduce our stress we should feel happier, right? It depends on what you believe.

This first approach to enriching one's life follows some degree of logic but is undermined by the belief itself. It is not possible to believe that life is difficult and then live an easy life. It is not possible to believe that life is painful and then live without pain. Inherent in the belief that life is suffering is our focus on evidence to support that same belief. We always make ourselves right when it comes to our beliefs and, therefore, we still feel stress instead of happiness.

Let's consider the second approach to life. This alternative approach acknowledges that life is perfect exactly as it is. Inherent in this belief is the idea that no matter what happens we can find evidence to see the perfection. Knowing that life is perfect reinforces our belief that no other judgment is necessary. We cease to look at life from a binary perspective. We let go of our belief that life has negative experiences. In other words, we acknowledge how we feel but without placing a judgment on those feelings.

The question then arises, which approach do you prefer to live with? One that says life is *hell* or that life is *perfect*? If you truly believe life is perfect and that you are fulfilling your purpose, you will not be feeling "bad"; instead, you will just feel what you feel—without the judgment. However, before you answer the question, consider which belief brings you the greatest joy in your life. While contemplating the question, be careful not to base your answer on *the past* or on your projection of what *the future* might hold. To answer honestly, stay focused only on this very moment and on nothing else.

You are probably thinking, "Well, at this very moment everything is just fine." Exactly the point! At every moment everything is perfect. When we tap our imagination or beliefs without a sense of purpose, our judgment determines that life is imperfect, difficult, and emotionally painful. The secret to living with joy is to string a series of perfect moments together in order to create the life we want.

For those of you who are skeptical about this approach, stop for just a moment and ask yourself, "Why do I believe that this is not a practical approach to life? Where am I selecting evidence to discredit this approach? Am I using only my experience at this very moment, or am I being influenced by an external source?"

A gentleman called when I was a guest on a radio talk show. He said that he was terminally ill with cancer and only had two months to live. When I asked him how he knew he was terminally ill, he said that two doctors had diagnosed his condition. I asked him again how he knew he was going to die. He finally admitted that he didn't know for sure that he was going to die. The caller was so externally focused that he had failed to acknowledge himself as the expert on his own life. He later revealed that he had already exceeded the life expectancy first diagnosed by his doctors. Unfortunately, as a result of his belief that he was terminally ill, he began to prepare his will and in the process began to increase his anger toward certain family members who he felt had not supported him. He now had another set of beliefs that he was adopting about how bad and wrong some of his family was. It had never occurred to him to take inventory of his own beliefs and how they were influencing his life. I asked him what the difference was between being terminally ill and being terminally well. He was so invested in his resentment and illness that he ignored the question, and I suppose he chose to believe he was terminally ill. Did he die happy or miserable? I don't know, but I think it is more important to ask if he *lived* happily or in misery.

Modern medicine is a wonderful gift, and when we complement our terminal wellness with medicine, we more clearly recognize the perfection of our being. We no longer look at doctors as the experts in our lives but, instead, as assistants who can support us in fulfilling our mission in life. After all, any physician is only as effective as the patient's willingness to live true to his or her purpose.

Those of us who have witnessed the death of someone near to us often enter a state of judgment because of our own beliefs about how long we wanted that person to live. What I have realized is that when people die, they leave us with a reason to celebrate. If we choose to believe that people die having fulfilled their purpose, we might celebrate their success. Our level of comfort or discomfort around death is determined by what we choose to believe. In my book *The Essence of Living* I wrote about the philosophy of energy and the concept of energy transformation. From this perspective, we recognize death as merely a transformation of energy and not necessarily an end unto itself. Viewing death in this context helps people avoid judging death as bad or good.

In the ecocycle of life, we all serve a purpose that some believe is beyond our comprehension. As humans, we sometimes fail to see the intricacy of the planet. In our arrogance, we believe that we are the single most important entity on the planet. We don't realize that our life experiences have no more and no less meaning than that of the planet itself. Our responsibility to ourselves is to live in a way that is consistent with our individual purpose. While this may seem selfish to some people, we must realize that our individual purpose is also a common purpose shared by other members of the ecosystem. For most of us, that means we want to feel content, peaceful, loving, connected, or just plain great!

So what happens in the process of creating what we think we want? To answer this question, we must examine the beliefs that support our reasoning. In the case of relationships, we might have an initial belief that a companion will help us feel fulfilled. The secondary belief may establish expectations about the relationship. The moment our expectations are not met we immediately believe that we will not be fulfilled. As we imagine how terrible our lives might become, we begin to find evidence to support that belief. A third belief then emerges and we may say, "This relationship is detrimental to my happiness." Again, we will find evidence to prove how the relationship is making us miserable. The mounting evidence to support our beliefs results in a shift in our behavior. We behave, not with the intention to share joyfully with our partner, but on our reaction to the belief that suggests we are at risk. As you can see from this scenario, there are contradictory beliefs about the relationship. The subsequent beliefs about the relationship obviously do not serve to satisfy the initial intention to experience personal fulfillment.

We typically follow a similar sequence of thoughts and beliefs that undermine our fulfillment in other areas of our lives as well. In order to interrupt the pattern of conflicting beliefs, we must first understand what happens in our thought processes. With this understanding, we might find the explanation for why we often have plans and good intentions that seem to go unfulfilled or that backfire. For example, some people may decide to have a few drinks to relieve stress and relax. After drinking, they may wake up the next morning feeling hung over. Now they must go to work feeling ill or call in sick. The fact that they are not able to perform to their standards may generate thoughts about the possibility of losing a promotion, being replaced, or even fired. Now feeling insecure about their position, they may try to overcompensate or cover up their hangover to avoid the dreaded fate of unemployment. The resulting behavior may be that these people lie, become aggressive, or withdraw from interaction with others. Having alienated co-workers and possibly the boss, they now feel even more stress and perhaps even shame. The belief that drinking makes us feel better only perpetuates the cycle of more stress. The point of this example is to illustrate that our intentions do not always guarantee us the desired results, which in this case was to feel relaxed and calm.

Beliefs in Action

*The decisions and choices you make
directly affect your circumstance.*

One reason we don't often fulfill our intentions is because fear-based emotions get in the way. If you were to ask others why they were afraid, they would most likely say because they believe they are in danger of ultimately feeling pain or possibly death. This belief is usually based on their personal experience. A personal experience could be real or imagined. However, we also have emotions which seem to be unexplainable. We sometimes credit these emotions to intuitions, instincts, or mysticism. Someone might even explain, "I was possessed." Is it true that we are at the mercy of our random emotions? I don't think so!

In the statement "I don't think so" are the clues to our emotions. I have discovered that emotions are the result of our thoughts. However, there is a very important distinction that must be made. Not all thoughts lead to an emotion. The thoughts that we adopt as beliefs determine the emotions we feel. Once a thought is adopted as a belief we then designate that thought as real, and in response we get a feeling. That feeling then moves us to physically respond or behave in a certain way. For instance, if I think about winning the championship game, I may have other thoughts about how many points I would need to score and most likely would not have a strong emotional reaction. But if I convert that thought about winning the championship to an imagined belief that I have already won the big game, I might feel elated and joyful. My corresponding behavior might be to jump up and down while yelling, "We're number one!" Likewise, if I believe I will lose, I may feel inadequate, disappointed, or fearful about playing the game.

Our behavior creates situations, circumstances, or conditions that are either consistent or inconsistent with the *essence* of what we want and intend. Again, using the example above, if I jump up and down with joy, others may celebrate with me. If I slam my fist against the locker, I might feel physical pain and will probably alienate others with my offensive language. And just like the person who drinks to feel better, my intention to have fun by participating in athletics is undermined by an opposing belief that says, "I am a loser." So if our purpose is to feel joyous, then we must believe it is all right for us to feel joyous whether or not we win or lose the game. Maybe we can adopt a new adage that says, "It's not whether you win or lose; it's what you believe before, during, and after you play the game." When we realize the relationship between our thoughts, beliefs, emotions, and behavior, then we can assume responsibility for our feelings, actions, and circumstances.

Some people may say this theory is flawed because sometimes we are victims of the hostilities and aggressions of others. Consider the belief that says, "No matter what happens, I am never a victim." Yes, circumstances arise outside of our control. Many of the things that happen to us are not pleasant, but we still have the power to decide what beliefs we will choose to support our joy and well-being during those difficult times in our lives. Too many of us choose to focus on our unpleasant circumstances instead of choosing beliefs that allow us to focus on creating what we truly want. Since beliefs are self-fulfilling prophecies, when we focus on what we don't want or don't like, we continue to perpetuate the undesired circumstance or result.

Memories As Beliefs

The destiny of our history lies
in the future of our past.

We need to examine our beliefs around the subject of time. In particular, we need to consider the element of time called the past. We access the past through our memories. But what is a memory? It is simply a belief about how things once were or used to be. We must invoke the creativity of our imagination in order to reconstruct the past. The use of our imagination can be very powerful. We use our imagination to recall the past in the form of painful or joyful memories. In our remembrance, we can never create the scene exactly like it was. We can only create the scene as we imagine it was.

Many people want to argue this point by saying that their memories are real. This is exactly the point. We create very real experiences for ourselves purely in our imagination. Someone might respond and show me a healed wound and say, "Tell me this scar is not real." Yes, the scar is real as we see it in its physical manifestation. However, the event that caused the scar only exists in the mind of the person remembering the event *now*. Since the wound is not being inflicted at the present moment, we can only assume that the memory of the event is a product of imagination. Is it possible to imagine the event differently that created the scar?

This depends on what you choose to believe. If you believe we can use our imagination to create a different memory of a past event, then you could create your remembrance of the event to be less painful. If you don't believe it is possible to imagine the event differently, then you may be stuck with painful memories. As you can see, believing in the limitations of our imagination only perpetuates our current reality in a way that may not bring us joy and happiness. This kind of limiting belief creates a detour that denies us our purpose.

I was speaking to one person who said that I needed to attend personal growth workshops. When I asked why she believed I should go to the workshops, she said that I seemed entirely too happy, and that I must be covering up my pain. I inquired about how attending such workshops would benefit me, and the response was, "You'll resolve old issues and you will be happy." This person had been so indoctrinated with the belief that we can't create our own happiness that she could not see the possibility for us to empower ourselves.

Some people who subscribe to the belief that no one has a perfect life promote the idea that if we don't acknowledge at least some painful memories, we deny our past and suppress our feelings. The memories that create anger, sadness, or depression we supposedly conceal and, hence, harbor as discord in our minds and bodies. Generally, we don't think of ourselves as suppressing fond memories. When we have memories that we enjoy, we usually smile, laugh about times gone by, and feel good. We typically attribute these feelings to our present state of being at that moment. If we feel happy at the moment, does it mean we are concealing pain? If we are feeling pain, does it mean we are concealing happiness? Perhaps painful and joyful feelings are just products of our imagination or the beliefs we hold at that moment. The feelings we generate from our current beliefs may be the only feelings that ever exist for us. If this is true, then it is unclear to me how the belief in suppressed feelings supports us in creating the joy that we want in our lives today. Is there really such a thing as a repressed feeling, or are our feelings just a reflection of our present beliefs?

It depends on what you believe. If you believe that feelings are these mysterious impulses that have a mind of their own and attack us like parasites, then this concept may seem very real to you. However, if you believe that feelings are a by-product of your beliefs, then you probably experience only those feelings that you have chosen to create in your imagination. By believing that we have repressed feelings, we set the foundation for manufacturing evidence that proves the belief. The significant question to ask is, "Does creating repressed feelings bring us our greatest joy or do we actually experience joy and peace by focusing on our purpose in the present moment?"

It depends on what you believe. If you believe that spending a lifetime reinventing imagined and painful stories about your past is bringing you your greatest joy, then you are probably fulfilling your purpose. If you believe that reinventing the past in search of painful memories is a waste of time, then you are probably a person who creates joy in your every activity, including reading this book. Congratulations! You are fulfilling your purpose!

Chapter 4

Believing without Risk

When we begin to understand our own purpose, then we can begin to see the fulfillment of our desires.

How do we actually change beliefs? The most common way is subconsciously through our experiences and through programming from external influences. If we wish to create exactly what we want, we must be able to change our beliefs consciously. In your own life, can you think of a belief you once had that you no longer have?

I remember that as a child I believed in Santa Claus. I was sure there was an old, jolly, fat man dressed in a red suit who would actually show up on Christmas Eve with a bunch of reindeer and then slide down the chimney just to leave presents under a tree. I can't remember when I stopped believing that he could fit down the chimney, but

I don't believe that he can. Not all children believe in Santa Claus. Depending on their religion or cultural traditions, there are probably other things that they once believed as children that they no longer believe. Why did I stop believing in Santa Claus? I think because I was told there was no Santa Claus and because there were never any dirty footprints leading from the fireplace to the Christmas tree. Also, I eventually discovered a reasonable explanation for how the colorfully wrapped gifts ended up under the tree—thanks, Mom and Dad!

Are reasonable explanations enough to cause us to change our beliefs? In fact, modern science has played a significant role in modifying our beliefs. Sailors once believed the earth was flat. Very few people still believe the planet is flat. Can you imagine how limiting it might be if you still believed the earth was flat? Some beliefs serve to enrich our lives and we tend to discard the ones that don't. We have the inherent power to imagine and believe whatever we want.

I think we can each find evidence in our lives of how we have changed our beliefs. Since we have demonstrated to ourselves that we have the power to choose or change our beliefs, we can simply exercise our choice to believe in those things that bring us joy, happiness, and great feelings.

Why do any of us select a different belief? Generally we find that updating our beliefs will enrich our lives in some way, even if it is by avoiding what we don't want. All of our experiences in life are a result of how we assess our situation at that moment. We often take an infinitesimal fraction of time and judge our lives in one thought. In that fraction of a second, we decide to believe our lives are working well or that we have problems. We fail to realize that in the next instant the picture of our lives may look different. Most of us don't look at our lives as a motion picture, where the multitudes of frames roll by to create the story of our lives; instead, we put the movie projector on freeze-frame and say, "Look how my life turned out."

The Earth Speaks

I was flat because they said so,
I am round because they believe what they say,
I rotate because they experience repetition,
I orbit because someone always sees the light,
I die when I become what they are,
I live because they do not understand
my mystery or their own.

Diminishing Risk in Your Life

The largest mountains for us to climb
are the ones we create in our own minds.

Many people resist discarding a belief because they have discounted the power of their imagination. Since many of us view change as a risk, we feel more secure believing that we are better off with things as they are. This perspective only serves to limit the opportunities we could otherwise create for ourselves. For example, many people will stay in uncomfortable jobs and relationships because they don't see the possibilities to create the life they truly want; they have no sense of purpose or commitment to a vision. Often if you ask people in this situation what they want, they will most likely tell you what they don't want. In other words, their attention is not on what they are creating in their lives. This is an example of an avoidance strategy. However, when we have a commitment to our purpose, we are less likely to stay attached or become dependent on our existing reality if it is not fulfilling our purpose.

For many, reality is based in fear, but fear is a product of our imagination that we choose to believe as real. Our imagination generally leads us to believe that we are on the verge of rejection, abandonment, pain, or death. The belief that these things are imminent causes us to be alert and focus on any sign that provides evidence that we are in immediate danger. As we become increasingly afraid, we are simply unable to fulfill our purpose. We sometimes even forget that we have a purpose and, therefore, can't find evidence that supports anything other than our fear, which leads to anxiety, stress, loneliness, anger, frustration, sadness, depression, and other unpleasant feelings. Not until the discomfort from fear becomes too intense do we consider confronting and replacing our fear-based beliefs.

The notion that we can overcome fear is a bit misleading. Fear is not something we overcome; we merely shift our imagination and focus instead on what we want to create at the present moment. This causes us to take action. We move from being reactive to being proactive: We decide to divorce or to be more loving in our relationships, or we decide to be more assertive at work or to get a new job. When I hear people complaining and blaming, I am certain there is a fear-based belief in operation. Truly purposeful people are busy taking proactive steps to create the *essence* of what they want. Reactive people stay bogged down in self-pity or try to make others the scapegoats for their own problems.

Perhaps you are still assessing the risk of changing a belief. What is your belief about the risk? Risk is nothing more than a fear-based belief. Is changing your beliefs to create a happy life really a risk? As you explore the risk, are you focused on fulfilling your purpose? Of course not! Therefore, contemplating the risk does not assist you to fulfill your purpose. What is the risk of holding on to your current beliefs? Will your life be better, the same, or worse? Some people are skeptical or are simply afraid of what they might discover about themselves. Maybe now is the time to discard your belief about the risk of discarding beliefs! Any belief that creates fear—in the form of risk or lack of trust in our purpose—inherently keeps us from experiencing our *essence*.

Let's check in with your emotions. When you believe that there is a risk, how do you feel? Is the feeling consistent with the *essence* of what you want? Probably not! I've never met anyone who prefers fear over feeling comfortable and free. However, I have met people who prefer excitement over calm. Some people even confuse fear with excitement. These individuals believe that by confronting their fear through living dangerously, they are creating the *essence* of what they want. Actually, this is an artificial way to get the sensation of excitement. They don't believe they can experience the emotional high in "normal" life situations. They become addicts of their own adrenalin rush from external stimulation or they rely on artificial stimulants, such as drugs and alcohol, to create a high feeling. Why engage in activities that endanger well-being for the sake of an adrenalin high? When we find excitement in our daily lives without jeopardizing our well-being, then we can begin to fulfill our true purpose.

Now focus again on your purpose. As you think about the beliefs that support your purpose, how do you feel? Perhaps you feel at ease and calm. Ask yourself which emotions you prefer and choose to experience. Do you choose the stress that comes with fear-based beliefs, or do you prefer the calm that comes with beliefs that support your purpose?

If you choose to retain your fear-based beliefs, you may also have other supporting beliefs that may cause you to feel undeserving of what you want. Often these types of beliefs originate during childhood. We do discard some childhood beliefs more easily, while staying attached to others. It is not uncommon for people to believe that they do not deserve to be happy, wealthy, healthy, or wise. Is it your purpose in life to feel undeserving? Of course not! So what is the risk in letting go of your undermining beliefs? **I have discovered that risk is only a belief about our inability to create what we want.**

Part Two

Mastering the Illusion

❖   ❖   ❖

Chapter 5

Designing Your Life

Without purpose, the wheel of life goes flat.

On the next page is a circle divided into eight compartments. This circle is what I call the *Wheel of Life*. How most of us get this wheel to turn is by compartmentalizing our lives and emphasizing certain areas of our lives at different times. When we feel one area is going well, we generally turn our attention to another area of our lives. This illustration shows how the *Wheel of Life* functions. First, you must fill in each compartment with your own definitions of the compartments you have in your life. Fill in the compartments in the order that they are numbered. As you write in the various compartments, remember to turn the wheel or page counterclockwise and begin writing from the center of the circle. Some examples of how we segregate our lives include relationships, family, children, social time, careers, finances, hobbies, spirituality, exercise, recreation, health, personal time, and the list goes on.

WHEEL OF LIFE

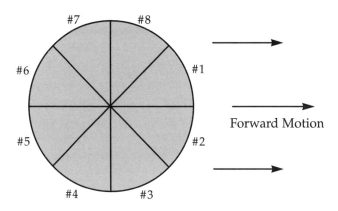

Forward Motion

After you have completed your entries, you will notice that you may have listed them in priority order. Also, notice which compartments are opposite one another: 1:5, 2:6, 3:7, and 4:8. What the *Wheel* illustrates is that when you are focused on compartment one, compartment five is upside down or out of focus. Think about your life and determine if, in fact, you live your life based on the compartments you filled in.

While the *Wheel of Life* model reflects how many of us live, it may not be the most effective way for us to fulfill our purpose. Once we have determined our purpose or *essence*, another option becomes obvious. We can focus on our purpose instead of on the various compartments of our lives.

Life's Third Dimension

Purpose is the center and balance of life.

The illustration below offers another perspective and dimension to the *Wheel of Life* that most of us do not consider. This new paradigm suggests that we not focus our lives on one compartment at a time but that we balance all aspects of our lives simultaneously. The new model looks more like a spinning top than a bicycle wheel. A bicycle wheel will turn even if it is out of balance. A spinning top will simply fall over if any one side is severely out of balance. The point is that we need to integrate and balance our lives if we are to spin on our axis or stay centered on our *essence* or purpose. Our *essence* is the core of our being, and we must allow all aspects of our lives to support our balance and our purpose.

NEW PARADIGM FOR THE WHEEL OF LIFE

Essence
(Core of your being)

Many people are not sure what having an integrated or balanced life feels like. To balance and integrate our lives, we must no longer look singularly from the viewpoint of each compartment. The following statement, "I love my job but my financial situation is terrible," shows how we can fragment our lives. Another perspective might be, "I love my job and I see many opportunities developing from this experience." In the first statement, the emphasis was not on what is being created but on the lack of adequate finances. The second statement acknowledges the possibility of using the job to generate greater financial resources. The issue is not the job or the finances, though; the issue is about how our focus and beliefs create comfort and joy. Does this mean that people's financial status may change instantly? Not necessarily, although it is possible. But by not having an attachment to the financial outcome, people stay open to possibilities by not creating stress over money. Also, they will not continue to find evidence that suggests they are on the verge of financial ruin. **When we focus on what we don't have, we are unable to create what we want.** We must realize that every aspect of our lives is available to assist us in fulfilling our purpose. In this respect, our lives become whole instead of compartmentalized.

The intention of compartments is to allow us to find areas of our lives where we can consider ourselves successful. Again, when we compare our lives to others or even against our own expectations, we sometimes miss the chance to acknowledge our true success, which is to fulfill our purpose and experience our *essence*. Since many people have not viewed themselves as successful, attractive, wealthy, and wise, they are not familiar with what it feels like to live with each of these attributes. Therefore, despite our successes, we still may not feel happy. Most people believe that once they are enlightened, successful, wealthy, married, and so on, their lives will look and feel totally different. From my observation, the only thing that really changes is how we experience and respond to the events in our lives.

For example, many people enjoy celebrating the Christmas holiday and the arrival of the New Year. They look forward with anticipation and expectation to experiencing a loving, joyful holiday season with family and friends. They also make resolutions for the new year, hoping to improve their lives. As the season arrives and passes, often their expectations are not met, and resolutions are broken. They then feel disappointed, guilty, and perhaps shameful when those expectations are not met. Their disappointment comes from judgments about themselves and how their holidays should be. Once they learn to fulfill their purpose, they can experience those same holiday events, including the breaking of a resolution, and still live their *essence*. The true opportunity for a shift in their lives does not come from their physical reality but from how they respond to it. In other words, when they believe and feel successful and happy, they actually create continued emotional success whether or not their physical environment meets their expectations.

Usually, we confuse our expectations and desires as essential to our existence. Many people perceive that they have basic needs beyond just food, shelter, and clothing. In life, we must be able to distinguish a need from a preference. In affluent societies, we seem to have lost a clear distinction between the two. There is nothing the matter with stating a preference, but if we confuse a preference with a need, we often find life to be disappointing and threatening. When we believe we need something, that belief goes into action, and we may feel our well-being is threatened if that need is not met. A preference, on the other hand, is not essential and, therefore, it is easier for us to let go of our attachment to the event, person, place, or thing.

Chapter 6

How to Create What You Want

*The purpose of your intention
is to help you realize how close you are
to what you want to accomplish.*

The formula for creating the *essence* of what we want is so simple that we miss the obvious. We must know what it feels like to have what we want; otherwise, we will not recognize that experience when it is upon us. How will you know you are truly happy if you don't know what truly happy feels like? How will you know true love if you don't know what true love feels like? Many of us rely on others to tell us how we should feel. Even if others don't know, they pass along what someone has told them or what they saw in a movie. It is no wonder many of us feel unsuccessful—we set unoriginal goals and expectations.

For instance, if you are creating from a space of originality, you may be writing the book you always dreamed about. Why are you reading this book? If you are looking for answers to your life, you may spend a lifetime searching. There are no questions to which you do not already have the answer. If you are searching for your *essence* external to your own beliefs, you most likely have not realized your *essence* or fulfilled your purpose. **To fulfill your purpose you must become an expert on the beliefs that create your reality.**

You cannot become an expert in your life until you believe you are an expert in your life. There are no legitimate "How to" books on becoming an expert: This book is only a reflection of my own experience and beliefs. Others have found value in adopting these beliefs as their own and maybe you will, too. All programs that offer solutions to enrich life, whether they have five, seven, or twelve steps, are no more or less valuable than any other. You must consider and decide which beliefs or combination of beliefs brings you closest to your *essence*. How you benefit from any belief or program is ultimately determined by how you integrate it into your life.

I have found a simple formula for reframing our problems and fear-based thoughts into a perspective that enables us to choose the *essence* of what we want. This approach works with any area in your life where you are dissatisfied.

Formula for Creating What *YOU* Really Want

Ask yourself these questions:

What issue am I concerned about?

What am I ultimately afraid of (abandonment, rejection, pain, death)?

What is the *essence* of how I want to feel (define the feelings you would prefer to have)?

Is there any factual evidence that the event I am afraid of is actually happening?

Other than believing in my fear, do I have a reason to be afraid right NOW?

Will you choose to think about your fear or choose to think about what you want NOW?

I choose _____

By using the above formula you may be able to realize that focusing on fear is precisely what generates our beliefs, emotions, behaviors, and, as a result, our life circumstances. The longer we believe that life is not perfect, the more evidence we mount to support that belief. When we take personal responsibility to select only those beliefs that bring us joy, we are propelled in the direction of evidence that supports our belief that life is wonderful.

Personal Responsibility

*The people who do not discover truth
for themselves will keep searching.*

Those who have a subconscious belief about their worthiness generally struggle with the concept of personal responsibility. Therefore, they meet with resistance the idea that they can change their reality and level of emotional fulfillment. Without having the permission from an authority (teacher, leader, guru, therapist, minister, expert, etc.), they do not believe that they have the personal power to create love, harmony, and joy in their lives. As a result, they continue to live life as if it were a movie that someone else wrote for them. Some people rely heavily on religion, mysticism, or professionals to help them find peace and happiness. Likewise, if you become dependent on this book, you may not yet realize your ability to be the expert on your own life.

In a sense, when these supporting relationships with authority figures take on a dependent quality, they invoke an avoidance strategy that perpetuates the belief that we are not complete or whole as people. By denying our intellect and the power of our beliefs, we exonerate ourselves from the responsibility to create the emotions we truly want. This denial allows us to continue finding evidence in our lives that life is a struggle. Those who believe that their personal growth journey is a lifelong process will no doubt be in a lifelong process of *trying* to create happiness.

When I want to create something in my life, I start with an idea or vision, like the idea to write this book. The idea becomes clear as I allow a physical image of the book to manifest itself in my imagination. Without getting attached to a specific physical manifestation of what I imagine, I can become familiar with what it feels like to have exactly what I want—a published book that helps people to empower themselves. Using my imagination, I then experience the feelings both emotionally and physically. I always pay close attention to how my body feels when I experience the *essence* of what I want. Once I memorize the feelings, I am able to reinvent them at my choosing, by simply accessing my imagination. I can choose to feel abundant, productive, worthwhile, creative, content, whole, peaceful, and so forth.

The more I feel the emotions that align with my vision, the more my physical reality starts to align with my vision. The book, for example, starts to take form as my sense of purpose and my emotional state compel me to write. Often my continued inspiration or motivation seems to come to me subconsciously when I am fulfilling my purpose. I totally trust in my ability to manifest or create the *essence* of what I want because I am already experiencing it spiritually. It is this absolute trust in my knowledge and perfection that deflects any fear-based thoughts that might come to mind about my inability to create what I want—to publish the book.

I dismiss any evidence that appears to undermine my success. What most people consider to be negative events, I simply address without placing any judgment, significance, or meaning on them. This allows me to stay focused on what I am creating and not be distracted from my purpose. Usually, I see the physical manifestation of what I have imagined within a very short time.

For example, I completed the initial manuscript for this book in just weeks. The physical manifestation of my vision is always consistent with the *essence* of what I want, although the physical form may sometimes look different than what I had originally imagined. Since I have no attachment to the appearance of the physical form, it does not matter to me how my vision is manifested as long as I experience the emotional payoff that is consistent with my purpose. In this way, my purpose is being fulfilled before, during, and after my vision and the physical manifestation of that vision. In this case, I feel excitement and joy from conceiving, writing, publishing, and marketing this book.

Beliefs About Change

In life there are no steps or processes to happiness. There are only steps and processes to changing your beliefs about happiness.

As we become personally aware of our beliefs and learn to influence our emotional state in ways that are consistent with our purpose, we must also be willing to accept change in our lives—without resistance. This is only possible if we have clear answers to the following questions: What is change? How do we measure change? How do we initiate and adapt to change? How does change affect us?

What is your definition of *change*? After some contemplation on this question, you may arrive at the answer. Many people have concluded that change is merely another perspective or point of view. So how do we perceive change? The answer may be viewed from a physical perspective or from the orientation of our beliefs. But our physical observations are sometimes a by-product of our beliefs—you know, the old we-will-find-evidence-to-prove-ourselves-right routine.

On the next page is an illustration of two circles. Each circle has a smaller circle inside the larger one. The larger circles represent how people approach change in their lives. In the first instance, people may choose to resist change and stay attached to current beliefs or a physical environment. They then feel like change is happening all around them. In the second case, people may avoid the perceived discomforts of change by taking action first. These people initiate movement in their lives and to them it appears that everything else stays stagnant.

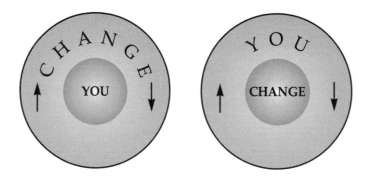

Move and the world will look different.

The third alternative is represented by the single circle above that integrates us into a whole life experience. In this case, we are not viewing change from the outside in or the inside out; instead, we become fluid with change. This means we simply accept our situations and circumstances as they are. I am not suggesting that we give up our purpose and the vision we have of our preferred lifestyle. I am simply emphasizing that when we focus on our *essence*, changes in our lives are directed toward fulfilling our purpose, instead of perpetuating what we don't want. The concept of becoming fluid with change can be explained using the following example:

> *Picture yourself driving down the highway. Alongside you is another vehicle traveling in the same direction and at the same speed as you are. When you look out your window, you notice that the people in the next car appear to be stationary. While you continue focusing on the people in the next car, there is no obvious change in the scenery. However, if you look out the opposite window, the scenery seems to be changing rapidly as you see trees and cars go by quickly.*

Becoming fluid with change means finding a pace of life and a lifestyle that give you the impression that you are in motion with your surroundings. When we refuse to choose another perspective, we call that resistance, and resistance creates discomfort. For example, the most difficult and sometimes dangerous way to step on an escalator or moving sidewalk is to come to a complete stop before getting on. If you keep moving at a pace that is close to the speed of the escalator, you can easily step on without losing your balance. The same theory holds true when entering a highway. If you come to a complete stop, it is more difficult to enter the flow of traffic. Our lives are very much the same way. We must determine where we want to go and then get into the flow instead of standing still.

We perceive change in our lives by comparing our reality to another place and time. We must either engage our memory or predict what the future will be like. Whenever we spend our energy comparing, our attention is not focused on creating what we truly want at that moment. How our lives used to be is really of no significance to what we want and what we can create today. The reason many people compare their present condition to the past or future is that it serves to validate the beliefs that they have about their present reality.

Beliefs About the Future

*The present moment goes by faster
than the past or future can be seen.*

To be fair with our perceptions of the past, we must also consider this illusionary element of time we call the future. We access the future in the same way we access our past, using our imagination to create a prediction or projection. Projections, like memories, are merely a product of our imagination that we adopt as beliefs. If we use our imagination to invent the future with beliefs that generate painful feelings, then we call this form of projection *fear*. If our projections generate wonderful feelings, we call this *fantasy*. So when do fears and fantasies become reality?

It depends on what you believe. Most people have different criteria for defining their reality. Fear is generally adopted immediately as reality, and the belief that our fear is real generates anxiety and stress. Most of us believe that fear-based emotions are more real than emotions resulting from our fantasies. For example, if I asked you to close your eyes, take a deep breath, and imagine your most significant fear, you would begin to feel stress. After you open your eyes, you would most likely still feel the stress, frustration, confusion, or anger from your imagined experience. Sometimes when people imagine their experiences with an estranged spouse or an awful boss, they become victims of their memory of those experiences. As they relive the experience in their minds, their emotional state moves them further away from their *essence* and in the direction of their pain. Why? Because they believe that the painful experience could happen again. In a sense, their memory has predetermined their present and future reality.

Now, take another deep breath and then close your eyes while exhaling. With your eyes closed and your body feeling relaxed, imagine your perfect world where you can have anything you want, where you feel only the most wonderful emotions derived from loving relationships, job satisfaction, perfect health, financial abundance, and a sense of freedom where you can live exactly as you want in every moment. Can you allow yourself to imagine such a perfect life? (Hint: *It depends on what you believe!*)

Once you have imagined your perfect life, pay attention to how it feels physically and emotionally to get everything you ever wanted. Before you open your eyes, very gently kiss the back of your dominant hand and then softly rub the back of your hand against your cheek and quietly say to yourself, "I love you!" As you appreciate yourself, check in with your emotions to see how you feel as a result of your fantasy. For a short time, you may still revel in pleasant emotions—until you dismiss your fantasy as being real. As you can see, our emotional state will either align with our fears or fantasies, depending on what we choose to believe at that moment. An emotional state sometimes has less to do with our actual physical reality than it does with our projections of what we believe will happen in the future.

Reality is only a concept.

Chapter 7

Let Your Imagination Work for You

*True greatness is recognizing that your
purpose is imagined, not performed.*

Once upon a time, in a faraway land that was as close
as my office, I explored my imagination:

*I don't remember what day it is. I guess it really
doesn't matter. There is a calm in the air that surrounds
me. Everything seems so peaceful and still. I am
embraced by beautiful colors of fallen leaves that lie dor-
mant on the moist green grass outside my window. The
blanket of gold and brown leaves brightens the otherwise
cloudy day. I can feel energy moving through my body.
My fingers tingle with electricity. There is a warmth
that I notice in my abdomen and lungs. I radiate with*

peace and quiet joy. I am vibrant and my soul shimmers. I cause the particles around me to ripple like a stone that awakens the stillness of a reflecting pond.

My thoughts focus on my present state of being. Occasionally my bliss is interrupted by thoughts about where I am and who will believe that any of this is real. My thoughts shift again to the humming sound of the disk drive in my computer. I imagine the sound to be that of a stream generously flowing over rocks and through the woods. From over my right shoulder a gentle hand strokes my right cheek with a velvet tenderness. I cannot see the hand, but I know it is a hand that belongs to my very real imaginary world. My body feels light and buoyant. I enjoy floating on air. I feel nurtured and comfortable lying on the invisible cotton clouds overlooking the fallen leaves below.

In the distance a bird sings to me a melody so perfect that I can't repeat it. I smile with delight and appreciation for this magnificent creation and moment. The phone rings, and as I answer, my peace is not disturbed. A wrong number does not keep me from retaining the feelings that fill my being. It is part of my perfect reality. I choose for it to be this way. I choose for it to be this way. I choose for it to be this way. I choose for it to be this way.

With all the problems in our lives and in the world, we can still create happiness in our lives simply by using our imagination. It is our choice to focus on our problems or to focus on our purpose. The challenge for most of us is to discount the significance of our physical reality. Most of us, instead, discount our spiritual fantasies as real because we hold the belief that fantasies are too good to be true. Therefore, we sometimes only honor the physical manifestation of our fantasies as being real. And since we believe no one has a perfect life, we don't acknowledge the feelings that we have that make our lives perfect (self-fulfilling prophecy).

So how can you retain the feelings that you created in your fantasy on a moment-to-moment basis? The first place to start is by choosing the belief that says, "My life is perfect." Most people would then respond, "I'm not going to say that. I would be lying! My life isn't perfect." As you can see, the belief supports not having a perfect life. The reason most people resist believing they have a perfect life is because they believe that to have legitimate emotional joy we must simultaneously see the physical manifestation of what we believe brings us joy.

For example, in your fantasy you might have imagined having a luxurious house overlooking the ocean. While you were imagining living in the house, you may have had wonderful feelings of success, freedom, and perhaps peace. At that very moment, when you felt all those wonderful feelings, you were fulfilling your purpose. You actually believed you were in the house of your dreams. By focusing on those feelings and becoming familiar with them, you now know what it feels like to have a dream house overlooking the beach.

You may now realize that to have the feelings you want, you don't actually need to own the house. However, when we look around at our immediate surroundings, we don't see the physical house that we imagined and so we immediately say to ourselves, "Those feelings weren't real." This statement is an undermining belief that reinstates the feelings of mediocrity or the sense of emptiness in our lives. To maintain a feeling state that we want, we must always rely on our imagination. We will either use our imagination consciously or subconsciously to our benefit or detriment. In either circumstance, the feelings that support our purpose are as real as the feelings that don't.

For instance, I have taken several cruise vacations in

the Caribbean. About halfway through the week, I usually hear someone say, "Only a few more days and then it's back to the real world." This is a perfect example of how we often dismiss the beauty of the present moment to imagine what we don't want. It also illustrates how we don't associate an ideal lifestyle with our reality. If these vacationers could admit to themselves that they can create their perfect reality, they would begin to recognize how they fulfill their purpose at home or on vacation. When I take a relaxing vacation, I imagine that my life is and always will be relaxing. By focusing my attention only in the present moment, and on my relaxed state, I avoid projecting what I might feel like in the future.

Remember, we will always find supporting physical evidence to confirm our beliefs. To the vacationer who denied believing that a perfect and leisurely lifestyle was real, the physical evidence to prove that it was not real was an airplane ticket back home. But to me, the evidence that my leisurely vacation and lifestyle are real is the fact that I am creating what I want, which is to feel relaxed. The moment we dismiss or invalidate an imagined feeling, we simply experience the emotional state that relates to our next belief. If that belief does not support our purpose, then we must choose to discard that belief and focus on only those beliefs that cause us to feel the way that we prefer.

Attachment to Physical Proof

*The person with sight is blind to how much
is spent on the visual aspect of desire.*

One of the reasons people resist using their imagination and beliefs to alter their reality is because they relate to the world from only a physical perspective. They have not learned how to integrate their spiritual and physical reality.

In the physical world our imagination does not change facts—it only changes the way we respond to the facts.

For example, if we were to come upon a bridge that did not look sturdy, the chances are that it might not be. Using our imagination in this situation will not make the bridge any more secure. Many of us would feel great disappointment and complain about the inconvenience of having to find an alternate route. What is the purpose of crossing the bridge? (No, not just to get to the other side.) Why did we want to get to the other side? We are probably on our way to a place or to a person who we believe will bring us pleasure. If pleasure is the purpose, then crossing the bridge is not essential—feeling pleasure is.

To fulfill our purpose, we can acknowledge our initial disappointment about the bridge, but the next belief needs to be focused on our purpose or pleasure. Is it possible to feel pleasure even though the bridge is not passable? It depends on what you believe at that time.

When we place too much importance on or become attached to the physical form that we expect, we often do not recognize that what we want already exists in our lives. For instance, I hear people speak specifically about an object or person that they want. As they visualize having the thing that they want or being with the person they want, they also become attached to seeing that object or person manifest in their lives. If something or someone else enters their life, they would dismiss the possibility that this was, in fact, what they were wanting.

What we must realize is that our expectations of the physical form do not matter. What is important is that we experience the feelings we want. If I enjoy being in the forest, does it really matter if I am in Oregon, Washington, California, or Colorado? Of course not! However, during my meditation or visualization, I may have imagined being in Colorado. By staying unattached to the physicalness of my vision, I can allow myself to be open to visiting another state or country and to experience the exact feelings I want.

When I lived in a suburb outside of Dallas, Texas, I experienced freeway traffic jams, long lines at restaurants, very long drives to scenic forested areas, and even farther distances to an ocean beach. I decided I wanted a lifestyle and quality of life that included an area that was sparsely populated, esthetically pleasing, and easily accessible to many outdoor activities. I had found several locations throughout the country that met my criteria and which captured the *essence* of what I wanted. Without an attachment to any one place or specific time frame, I was open to moving to any of the locations that I had discovered. Meanwhile, I began to imagine living in a location like the ones I had identified. I imagined myself working at home, setting my own schedule, enjoying the ambiance of the mountains, trees, and ocean. Through my imagination, I was able to experience what it felt like to live the life I wanted. At that point, I was already getting what I wanted, even while I was still living in the big city. One year later, I purchased a house in Oregon and ten months after that I moved from Dallas. My life is exactly as I chose to create it.

Integrating Imagination into Real Life

*Imagination is sometimes knowledge
looking for reality.*

When I go into bookstores, I usually see small books of daily affirmations near the cash register. These affirmations are reminders to us to acknowledge the beauty and power of our being. In a sense, we are asked to use our imagination to experience the affirmations as real. What I have discovered is that affirmations are not effective unless we actually believe the affirmations to be true—in which case we don't need these little books or the affirmations.

Likewise, if we use affirmations to try and convince our-selves that our lives can be better, then affirmations have little benefit.

Here is a simple and inexpensive approach that I use to apply imagination in my life: I pick any aspect of my life and imagine the *essence* of what I want. Once I know what I want, I sometimes have a conversation with myself to bring clarity into my own life or to enhance my relationships. In this process, I ask myself questions and listen to my imme-diate response. This allows me to tap into my intuition when I feel ambivalent or unsure about something.

I have also used the dialogue process to connect with those who are either physically or emotionally distant. Children use this same technique when they animate their favorite stuffed animal or doll. In my case, I use my imagi-nation to visualize the other person. I try to include as much detail as possible about where they are and what they look like. When I have a clear picture of them in my mind, I have a mental conversation with them. Since I am using my imagination, I can create the conversation exactly as I want it to be—instead of how I think it might actually be.

This process shifts my emotional energy to align with my purpose and in some way also seems to transfer to the other person. I even use a similar approach in business. I remember being asked by my employer to fly to Australia. One of our customers was irate over the performance of a machine purchased from our company. The poor perfor-mance of the equipment was costing our customer lost productivity and revenue. The local management of our subsidiary in Sydney was unable to negotiate a settlement with our customer.

When I arrived, I was told that the customer was being unreasonable and extremely hostile. When I met the top executive, he was very cold and apparently suspicious. The *essence* of what I wanted was to have a harmonious and productive meeting with the customer. While in the meeting, I imagined holding his heart in my hand and stroking it tenderly and lovingly. My intention was to calm his fears and build his trust. He almost immediately became more open and communicative. We worked out an agreeable plan of resolution. The general manager of our subsidiary commented with astonishment that he had never seen this executive be so reasonable and cooperative.

When we are not operating from fear-based beliefs, we do not become defensive, resistant, hostile, retaliatory, or resentful. As a result, people feel trusting and become more open and honest in their communication with us. Ultimately, we benefit from supportive and fulfilling relationships. I believe that when we focus on the *essence* of what we want, we begin to align with our purpose. We start to believe in the possibility of living from another reality that is emotionally fulfilling.

Chapter 8

How You See It

*There is more to the flower
than the beauty of its appearance.*

Our physical reality is what most people believe defines our life experience. So we find ourselves in a dilemma because we are constantly trying to have a spiritual experience in the physical realm. In other words, we want physical proof or evidence that our spiritual experiences are real.

This may explain why some people have a double standard for how they define reality. They often judge their imagined beliefs differently. Painful memories or even fears are, for some reason, considered more real than our fantasies. As we've already discussed, we do not demand the same degree of physical evidence to support our fears as we do for our fantasies. Fears that are based on our memories seem real because someone can say, "I was there and experienced the physicalness of that past situation."

By definition, we cannot have a spiritual experience if we are focused on the physical manifestation of our experience. As explained earlier, we can only focus our attention on one set of emotions at any given time. Whatever we choose to focus on in our lives will affect our life experiences. If we focus on our purpose, we increase our chances of having experiences that we enjoy. Our insistence on seeing the physical manifestation of our fantasies automatically keeps us from having a lasting spiritual experience, and keeps us from believing that the experience is real. To maintain a spiritual state of being while living in our physical bodies, we must be willing to select those beliefs that support our desired spiritual experiences at all times.

By integrating our spiritual fantasies as beliefs into our lives, we begin to live from a spiritual state of being. Most of us are quite experienced at living from a spiritual state of being called *fear*. Instead of living in a state of fear, consider how life would be if we would choose to live from a spiritual state called *fantasy*. Our spiritual state of being would allow us to feel relaxed and peaceful. Our lives would change drastically because we would no longer feel the need to worry. We could actually just enjoy our daily activities in a relaxed state. Oh yes, we might have more free time because we wouldn't "need" to meditate for hours or go to self-empowerment workshops. In addition, we would save money if we no longer needed alcohol, drugs, cigarettes, and other addictive substances to help balance our insecurities or depressed moods.

Many people intermix their physical and spiritual realities regularly in the course of a day. Any time we turn on the television or watch a movie we enter into a world of imagination. As we become engrossed in the make-believe world we see on the screen, we begin to experience a shift in our emotional state. We laugh, cry, and feel frightened or elated based on our degree of belief. In actuality, our physical reality does not change as we sit in the same seat for sometimes two hours or more. In fact, we can be so deep in our imaginative or spiritual reality that we don't even notice the person sitting just inches from us.

The point is that we can imagine our reality to be different by watching a movie. We can also use our imagination without watching a movie. The movie is merely a reflection of someone else's imagination. The person who created the screenplay used his or her imagination with the intention of having you experience his or her imagined reality. We each have the power to influence others as well as ourselves, using our imagination. Unlike movies, our imagination never ends. We can use it to our benefit during every moment of our lives. However, the only reality that counts is the one that we choose to experience. So why not use your own imagination to benefit you in fulfilling your purpose?

If you are thinking that this all sounds too easy, could it be that your belief is that life is difficult, complicated, and full of problems? Why do you believe that life is difficult? Did someone tell you it had to be that way? Are you remembering all the struggles you have had? Did you watch the news on television? Did your doctor tell you that you were sick or terminally ill?

Yes, there is an abundance of proof that life is difficult. While you are busy focusing on, proving, and convincing yourself that life is difficult, you will not find evidence that life is a joyous, easy experience. Yes, there is an abundance of proof that life is wonderful as well. You must be willing to alter your beliefs if you want to see the wonder of your life.

Judging Your Reality

When possibilities turn into expectations,
we are no longer living with purpose.

"Oh I get it! This is one of those books about positive thinking." If you believe in the power of positive thinking, congratulations! But this book is not about positive thinking. This book is about relinquishing your judgments about your life as being positive or negative. I am specifically addressing how our beliefs can assist us in experiencing the feelings we would prefer, without judging them as positive/negative, good/bad, or right/wrong. Our judgments are entirely subjective and reflect only our own assessment of the situation in freeze-frame mode.

For instance, what is your judgment about grief? Is it a positive or negative emotion? Some people judge grief as a negative emotion because it is painful. Others consider grief to be a positive emotion because it helps us come to terms with our perceived loss so that we can ultimately experience joy.

The point is that it is unnecessary to even judge the emotion. People experiencing grief are only feeling what they are feeling at that moment. They believe that they have lost something or someone dear to them. They are entitled to acknowledge their perceived loss and feel grief for as long as they choose. When they no longer want to feel the pain, they will select a different belief that supports them in generating their next preferred emotion. Most judgments that we have in our lives generally do not support us in fulfilling our purpose.

One of the most prominent ways that we harbor judgments in our lives is by categorizing and comparing. When I hold book signings, people will often decide to buy my book based on how they categorize me. People ask if I am of a particular religious or political persuasion. I simply tell them that I subscribe to no labels; I ask them to use their awareness to know who I am and not what I am. Those who like to categorize and compare usually become subtly judgmental. Behind every category we hold in our minds, there are secondary beliefs that perpetuate our judgments with evidence to support our categories. These secondary beliefs set expectations and reinforce stereotypes. Once we have the image of a stereotype in our heads, our experience of the world has then been predetermined. Hence, categorizing is a form of judgment and can limit our ability to live free of stereotypes that often feel threatening to us. Without categories we would be left with mere descriptions and may be more open-minded. This would allow us to experience the world with a sense of wonderment because every moment we would encounter a fresh, new experience.

If you are outside or near a window, look at a nearby tree. Now find a piece of furniture made of wood. As you compare the tree with the furniture, what can you determine is the difference between the two? *It depends on what you believe.* The beliefs we have about how things are categorized in our lives shift our perspective and our experience of those things. For example, we could say the tree is made out of wood and the furniture is made out of the tree. We could call both of them a tree or both of them wood. However, you probably would treat the furniture differently if you thought it was a tree, and you would treat the tree differently if you thought it was just wood. As you can begin to see, how we label and categorize things affects how we view and treat them. Our words sometimes carry more meaning than being merely descriptive.

Categorizing Your Reality

*You can't control your life;
you can only influence how you experience it.*

When we categorize and stereotype our own lives, we have a tendency to become bored with life. We look at new opportunities and dismiss them by saying, "Oh, I've done that before." We fail to recognize that all the circumstances in our lives have indeed realigned themselves except for in our own minds. We assume, based on our own observations, which are filtered through our judgments, that the outcome will be the same as we have experienced it before. For example, if we meet someone who reminds us of an old girlfriend, boyfriend, or boss that we had a bad experience with, we might shy away from that person. Despite there being entirely different circumstances and people involved, we believe that the new acquaintance will cause us to re-experience the past. We enter a state of fear as we categorize the new situation as risky.

Categorizing leads to judgment, expectation, fear, and immobility. The people who seem to be the most successful and happy are those who stay open-minded and don't view life as a risk or a series of repeat performances. They are not limited by categories and stereotypes of others or themselves.

Like most of us, the cartoon character named Popeye sometimes labeled himself by saying, "I'm Popeye, the sailor man." He also often said, "I am what I am." The beauty of this second quote is that he identified with his human experience without filtering it through his nationality, gender, ethnic background, religious or political affiliation, sexual orientation, or professional association. He was not responsible for fitting into the stereotype of the groups that he could have identified with (American, white, male, heterosexual, sailor, etc.); instead, he was responsible for being who he wanted to be as an individual. Do you believe you can be who you truly are, or do you believe you need to be part of a group to feel accepted and safe? If you choose not to categorize people, you can feel comfortable in many more situations because you can relate to people based purely on your individual purpose and on their purpose.

My belief and awareness is that group consciousness is not a substitute for individual consciousness, and group esteem is not a substitute for self-esteem. While many people maintain that feeling part of a group can help them to feel better about themselves, I often observe that those same people often relinquish their personal responsibility to create what they want individually. Sometimes when we believe we are part of a group, we feel we must conform in order to protect our image and the group's image. In our lives, we can either focus on our image or on our *essence* and purpose.

DISCOVERING LOVE

Soaring through the heights of my imagination
Cascading into the rivers of my veins

Believing in mountains that overlook
the landscape of my soul
Flowing over my heart and spraying a misty dew

Pondering every drop of eternity that floats
for a moment
Evaporating into the atmosphere of my thoughts

Awakening the belief that life is of my creation
Invigorating my spirit to the peak of fragrance

Living in serenity and selfless majesty
I share with thee this love I know as real

Part Three

From Magic to Miracles

❖   ❖   ❖

Chapter 9

Beliefs That Create Success

*The greatest reward comes from
knowing your own value.*

D o you believe you can be successful without fame and fortune? What is your definition of success? For many years, I defined success from only a materialistic viewpoint. While I certainly enjoy the comforts of material items and money, I have discovered that my purpose is fulfilled in a nonmaterial form. When I fulfill my purpose, I believe I add value to other people's lives. I also believe that I will be compensated for that value. As you may notice, these beliefs are a form of expectation. However, you will also notice that there is no physical element to these expectations. By using the word *compensation*, I am not attached to the physical form of money or the amount of money that I will earn or not earn.

For instance, this book is not yet complete and I have not recognized any income from this project. As I look out my window at the beautiful scenery in my backyard, I realize my sense of freedom, peace, and joy. I also know that I would not feel any more free, peaceful, or joyous if I had millions of dollars in the bank. The point is that when we experience our *essence*, our materialistic reality becomes insignificant.

Some who would criticize this belief may offer a belief that suggests it is not possible to experience our *essence* unless we have some degree of material wealth and physical sustenance. Of course, we can always debate these kinds of philosophical questions. However, the purpose of this book is not to prove that someone else's belief is wrong. The purpose of this book is to share with you my awareness of how I use my own beliefs to fulfill my purpose and live a successful life. People have the responsibility, regardless of circumstance, to determine what beliefs will ultimately benefit them in living their *essence*.

Beliefs About Money

After the bills are paid, you still owe yourself.

The issue of money raises many beliefs. It seems to me that the predominant belief about money is that there is not enough or that we will lose what we have. We also like to blame rich people for hoarding all the money. While there are individuals who have disproportionate amounts of money, they are usually not holding that money underneath the mattress of their bed. What this means is that in capitalistic societies, money is usually in circulation in the form of loans, salaries, services, products, and so on.

Money is merely an agreed-upon form of transferring *perceived* value. If you believe you can transfer your value in other ways, you may not need money—or at least not as much money. Perhaps you may consider bartering instead. The point is that money is not a scarce commodity. It is merely pieces of paper and processed metal. The obvious challenge for most people seems to be how to trade their value for more paper and metal. Once again, if you believe that you have little value, you will receive little money. If you believe you add significant value, then you will notice that people will pay you for the perceived value that you add.

Many people don't understand how they add value to the lives of others. This is true for some people both professionally and personally. When I ask people how much they think they are worth, they struggle with the question. So I might reframe the question and ask how much value they believe they add to the lives of others. We must take inventory of our personality, experience, knowledge, awareness, intention, beliefs, and purpose to determine our true value.

Once we can acknowledge the ways in which we add value to the lives of others, then we will also begin to realize how much money they might exchange for our value. Many people have told me that they are worth whatever they are currently being paid. Some people have even said they should be paid two to three times their current salary. What I don't understand is why people even limit themselves. I believe my value is unlimited. I also believe my value is commensurate with how successful I am at fulfilling my purpose.

I don't only measure my value in the form of monetary rewards (as I once did). I measure my value in relation to how I feel about myself and my life. What I realize is that as long as I am fulfilling my purpose in everything I do, I create significant value for others. My purpose includes feeling free, creative, joyful, peaceful, and generous. The ways I am compensated for being in my *essence* are through money, intimate friendships, generosity from others, gifts, letters, and, most importantly, peace of mind, love, and perpetual joy.

Unfortunately, we allow money to control us instead of being aware of how our beliefs about money control us. When we believe that money is the only way that our value is recognized, we generally will not feel fulfilled unless we have money. However, in order to create abundance in life, we must feel deserving. By holding the belief that we are nobody until we have money, we set ourselves up to miss fulfilling our purpose. How is it possible to attract emotional wealth if we are not already wealthy in spirit?

Creating Emotional Wealth

Your true wealth resides in the value of those beliefs that serve your purpose.

People with healthy incomes, despite many of their comforts in life, still feel unfulfilled. I suppose I would prefer to be unfulfilled with money than unfulfilled without money. However, I choose to create happiness regardless of my financial status.

If we are unhappy, we will still be unhappy regardless of our financial status. We can't go to the store and buy a jar of unhappiness nor can we buy happiness. If we believe that money is scarce, then we will be afraid that there will not be enough. Any belief that generates fear also possesses the power to control us. Choosing the beliefs that allow money and other forms of compensation to flow through our lives is an important aspect of supporting our purpose.

Take a moment to consider your life and the ways that

you are being compensated. Think about both monetary and nonmonetary forms. Does your compensation include the emotional rewards that you want? If you aren't feeling fulfilled and successful, then you are probably out of alignment with your *essence* and not fulfilling your purpose. When your emotional and spiritual success is high, then you will discover the value of your being is far greater than what you can deposit in the bank.

In order for us to succeed, we may need to adjust our definition or beliefs about what success means to us. Success, like love, means different things to different people. The most significant component of success is the joy that we feel. Therefore, we must acknowledge joy as the indicator of our success. The more joy we feel, the more success we create and the more value we add to the lives of others. This is a simple formula, and I have never seen an unhappy person be joyfully successful. Have you?

Often people are not joyful about their success because of their underlying fear of rejection. They associate rejection with failure. Therefore, they constantly worry about how others will perceive them. Some people feel they must demonstrate their success by upholding a socially acceptable image to impress others.

I refer to this form of deception as adult theatrics because we act or pretend to be someone different than who we really are. When we live in a state of adult theatrics, we do not acknowledge our adulthood, and we continue to live in an adolescent frame of mind where peer and parental acceptance is paramount. In this case, we often avoid admitting to our unhappiness because we believe that we will be rejected if we appear sad, depressed, or lonely. When our fear of rejection kicks in, we stop seeing ourselves as successful. At that moment, we believe we don't deserve to have success and we feel insecure about what others might say or think of us. Using others to validate us is certain to undermine our success. We must find the trust and truth within our own beliefs in order to create and maintain our *essence* rather than our image. We each have the responsibility to set our own personal criteria for success that goes beyond our conditioned belief about money.

Chapter 10

What Is LOVE,
Anyway?

*True love can only be discovered by
those who are pioneers of the soul.*

Feeling great for most of us requires at least one belief—
that we are wonderful and lovable. It seems that more
people focus on *being* loved rather than on *feeling* love.
What this tells me is that they believe love is conditional,
based on the response they receive or expect from another
person. It also suggests that they focus primarily on finding proof that they are loved. To feel love requires no
proof. We usually do not feel loved, however, without the
supporting evidence to prove it. I have decided to feel
love in my life and let the proof appear unconditionally.

But what is this word called *love*? I have often asked
people how they would define or describe *love* to an alien

from another planet. If a Martian landed here on earth and asked you, "What is this thing you humans call *love*?"—how would you respond? What I have found is that each of us has a slightly different interpretation of the word *love*. It is not surprising that with so many interpretations and expectations, we often have a difficult time creating loving and lasting relationships. One thing is certain: Since we each know love to be different, we must accept our beliefs about love as being responsible for creating our own experience of love.

Surprisingly, there are some people who simply admit they don't know what love is. Others maintain love is when you care about another more than you care about yourself. Those who have felt hurt being in a relationship may think that love is painful. I am certain that these beliefs are not helping people to see themselves as the creators of love.

If love is a feeling, how would you describe this feeling to the Martian, and where would you say the feeling comes from? Some people measure the degree to which they feel love based on how much grief they would feel if the person they love were no longer present in their lives. This may explain why many people perceive love to be different between parents, siblings, children, friends, and romantic partners.

In exploring this question for myself, I have discovered that love is a state of appreciation and joy. When I am appreciative of myself and I choose to acknowledge the perfection of my being, I can share (not give) that perfection with everything in my life. The emotional payoff for me is not based on the fear of losing love but on what I am constantly creating. As a result, I choose to know love as an emotional state I experience with people regardless of their relationship to me.

How we share love or express appreciation is through silent admiration, language, and touch. I first remember hearing the phrase "making love" when I was young. As a youngster, I thought making love meant sharing love. Then I started listening to the radio and watching movies. My understanding changed because I thought that by having sex people could actually *make* love. Even though this sounds ridiculous to me now, many people still unconsciously believe that having sex is how they can manufacture love.

Painfully, many have realized that sex does not generate love. Sex generates physical arousal and perhaps a temporary moment of physical bonding. For those who insist that sex creates emotional bonding, I invite you to explore your beliefs on this subject. Do you believe emotional bonding comes from sex or perhaps from some other source such as the appreciation you share with your partner? Until we know how to create and share love in a non-sexual way, we may never know the fullness of love.

I often tell people when I am feeling appreciative that I love them. If I haven't known them very long, people frequently say, "How can you say that? You don't even know me." I always tell them that I am merely expressing how I choose to feel and that they are not the cause nor are they responsible for how I feel. This is normally followed with a look of bewilderment.

I believe love, happiness, hate, and sadness are merely belief choices that we make in our lives. Usually someone will ask, "What if a person does something bad to you, would you still love that person?" How I choose to feel is always my prerogative. But why would I want to spend my time imagining a scenario that does not support my joy in the first place? If someone does something "bad," I will deal with it at that time. What I have found is that the less I conjure up hurtful scenarios in my mind, the less I experience hurt in my life. The more I conjure up loving scenarios when I first meet people, the more I experience love.

While this seems like a rather easy and simple way to live with love, it escapes many people because of their definitions and expectations around love. What I have chosen in my life is *unconditional love*. What this means is that I project my appreciation and loving feelings onto all things in my life.

When I realize that I am not feeling unconditionally loving, I know that there is a belief that is blocking me from fulfilling my purpose. The first place I look is at the beliefs that create my fear and judgment. In almost every instance, I find that this is why I am not feeling connected, open, and loving. Once I realign with my purpose, I can recognize that others have a loving side that may be masked by their own fear. When I am aligned with my *essence*, I notice that other people become less fear-based and judgmental in my presence.

Once we have chosen to live with unconditional love, we don't have to feel unconditionally loving all the time. The possibility exists that you are still an unconditionally loving person who does not choose to feel loving at the moment. The only condition of unconditional love is love. Reserving judgment of ourselves always allows us the chance to reclaim our loving spirit without shame and guilt. **Remember, our emotions are the checks and balances for our beliefs.**

Relationship Beliefs

*How would you treat yourself differently
if you were in love with yourself?*

The single most difficult area in our lives seems to be caused by our beliefs about relationships. Despite the fact that we are in constant relationship with other human beings from the time we are born, we still struggle with how to create the *essence* of what we want. When I ask people about what qualities they want in their relationships, I have found that many people believe they don't know. Some people will start to describe the physical attributes of their preferred mate. They will even list a profession, interest, or hobby that they want from their partner.

A single man in his early forties said he was ready to get married, for the first time, if he could find the perfect partner. He described his perfect partner very superficially. Later in the conversation, I asked him if he was perfect. He replied, "Well, no! No one is perfect." So, I asked another question. "If no one is perfect, how would it be possible to find your perfect mate?" He quickly realized why he was still single—he had conflicting beliefs and expectations about relationships. No doubt, had the perfect woman married this man, she would have had a hard time being accepted by him since he believed no one was perfect.

A common belief is that if we find someone who likes to do the same things we do, then we will get along and we will be happy. Participating in activities together is a great icebreaker for relationships; however, I am sure you know people who like to do the same things but who don't get along. This is true with individuals who belong to the same social groups, companies, and teams, as well as other organizations. Obviously, it is not a common interest alone that creates harmonious relationships.

The essential ingredient in successful relationships is the self-awareness of what each person wants to create and share. In other words, each person must understand his or her purpose. In all cases, people who I have spoken with around the world all have had a similar purpose regarding their relationships. They generally have wanted to share, communicate, be open and honest, laugh, trust, and have fun. Their emotional payoff or purpose has been to feel loving, connected, peaceful, comfortable, and happy.

A problem arises for those people who have not yet figured out how to be happy. It is virtually impossible to share joy with someone who is unhappy. The reason is that unhappy people are focused on their unhappiness. If we focus on our own or other people's unhappiness long enough, we begin to believe that we cannot create happiness in our relationships or other areas of our lives. The evidence to support beliefs about unhappiness can become overwhelming.

As is often the case, people meet others they believe to be wonderful during the courtship, but once married, they encounter difficulties. I have found that this common phenomenon is tied almost exclusively to our individual beliefs about marriage. Many people get married with loving intention but unsuspectingly undermine their relationship with their unconscious beliefs. These beliefs include expectations about gender roles, communication patterns, money management, lifestyle choices, spirituality, parenting, and even beliefs about their own self-worthiness and whether or not they deserve happiness. It is not uncommon for those who grew up in tumultuous, broken, or abusive families to believe that it is not possible to be happily married.

I have several friends who have never been married and who resist the idea partially because they claim they have never seen a happy relationship last. I believe that if we worry about our relationships not working, we do not actually focus on what we truly want to create with our partners. I once had a partner who often stated that our relationship was never going to work. I cautioned that such beliefs generate supporting evidence. In fact, as she became worried about the relationship not working, she also became unhappy, which only reinforced her initial belief. Not until we take inventory of our current beliefs will we be able to determine which ones allow us to experience true harmony with those we care about.

I frequently hear other people saying that they have problems in their relationships. They seem to believe that the *relationship* is an entity unto itself. I explain that the relationship is like a computer network. In order for the network to be effective, there must be at least two functioning computers on each end. This means that the quality of the relationship is only as enjoyable as the people who are involved. If either person is not capable of fulfilling his or her individual purpose, there is little chance that the network between the two will create love, peace, and joy. The relationship, like a computer network, is merely a communication vehicle for what each person is already creating in his or her life and what he or she wants to share. However, if one computer is not fully functioning and able to communicate, it doesn't mean that the network and the other computer are necessarily inoperable.

I was speaking with someone who said she was not happily married. When I asked why she believed that she was not happy with her marriage, she said the relationship had communication problems. Her belief was that if her spouse was listening and hearing her, she would see at least some changes in behavior. The degree of love and happiness this person felt was actually tied to an anticipated response to a previous conversation. Since her spouse did not respond as expected, she concluded she was not loved, and thus, unhappily married. This person never explored the belief that her spouse loved her unconditionally or that she could love her spouse unconditionally. She assumed that the network (relationship) was not working and, therefore, decided that the computer (her husband) on the other end was also shut down. Does believing that we are not loved or lovable help us to create loving relationships? When we believe that we are unhappily married, is it possible for us to still live happily? *It depends on what you believe.* In this instance, there was a series of beliefs that began to mount as evidence that happiness could not be shared in the marriage.

To enhance our relationships we must first acknowledge our own purpose and also realize that other people have a similar purpose. After all, no one really wants to have unhappy relationships. When we recognize that others also have a loving purpose, we can adjust how we relate to them. We can assist them in discovering what beliefs are not allowing them to fulfill their purpose. If our beliefs are, in fact, expectations of how other people *should* respond or *should* behave, we may be disappointed and become unhappy. This happens frequently in relationships where the condition for sharing love is based purely on physical attraction or preconceived behavioral roles.

Our feelings of disappointment indicate to us that our expectation about the situation may be out of alignment with our purpose. In other words, our purpose is to feel harmony and not disappointment. Therefore, we must examine what belief generates disappointment. Perhaps the belief that people must always be physically attractive or that their behavior will change quickly is what leads to expectations and ultimately our disappointment. The belief that generates the disappointment is not consistent with the joy we would prefer to feel or share with our relationship partner. Therefore, we must at least consider discarding those beliefs that do not bring us joy.

Many people believe that the more physically attractive someone is, the happier we will be with them in a relationship. The subject of attraction is tricky because we often are attracted to those who meet the socially acceptable standard of beauty. We are influenced heavily by the media and also our previous experiences with those we have loved. In many respects, our attractions are just another set of beliefs that we anticipate will bring us much joy. I have met many people who are so attached to a particular type of physical appearance, personality, profession, athletic ability, interest, and/or social status that they do not believe they can share in loving relationships with those who do not fall within their narrowly defined criteria.

By letting go of our beliefs about how others create our happiness, we start to open our minds to the possibility that we are already happy. Once we are happy, we can begin to share in loving relationships with a wider variety of people. As long as we hold others responsible for making us happy, then we will tend to blame them for our unhappiness. We may have a tendency to find fault with those who are intimately involved with us. Not until we commit to our purpose will we see the opportunity to choose a happy reality for ourselves. Once we discover how to imagine the ultimate feelings we want and prefer, then we will inherently begin to focus on our purpose.

For example, I heard a woman say about her boyfriend, "If he really loved me, he would call more often." Inherent in that statement is the belief that she is not loved because he does not call. A secondary belief supports the first belief as she begins to use her imagination to explain why he doesn't call. If the secondary belief is that she has been rejected or perhaps abandoned, she may then create a third belief. The third belief may be that she will never find anyone who really loves her. As she continues to use her imagination, each of these beliefs becomes a fear. Her emotional response to these beliefs or fears may result in anger, sadness, loneliness, depression, and disconnectedness.

By choosing to believe that phone calls determine her level of worthiness, she also begins to build evidence that suggests she is not worthy of love. Without considering any other possibility for why her boyfriend does not call, she uses her imagination to create unhappiness. In a sense, she is blaming him for creating her unhappiness. By simply selecting a different set of beliefs and imagining the situation differently, she could have easily created and shared joy in her life with her partner. Which is more important, his calling or her feeling joyful about herself and her life? Or both? Perhaps when she realizes her own joy, he will call more often.

In the above example, her beliefs can't actually make her boyfriend call more often, but they can influence how she responds when he doesn't call and when he does call. In one instance, her happiness is held hostage by the frequency of her boyfriend's phone calls. In the other case, her happiness is not dependent on his calling. But because she remains a joyful person, he and others prefer to call her more often. By staying committed to fulfilling her purpose, she not only uses her imagination to stay joyful but also to witness the physical manifestation of her desires—to have him call frequently.

I believe that all people must be personally responsible for creating only what they want in their relationships. If you want peace, be peaceful. If you want love, be loving. If you want joy, be joyful, regardless of what the other person is creating. We must commit to our purpose and choose partners who know how to create the *essence* of what they want in their own lives. I have decided to live only with a mate who, like myself, focuses on creating love and harmony in every moment.

The *Bolen Law of Propulsion* applies to our relationships. If we are focused on our unhappiness and blame others, we are propelled convincingly in the direction of evidence that supports our continued dissatisfaction. Beliefs are like a self-fulfilling prophecy. The more we focus on beliefs that create joy, the more we realize joy in our lives. As long as we believe in ourselves and the power of our creativity, we can choose to focus on what we want and live our *essence*.

Chapter 11

Living Beyond the Drama

*There is no greater drama
than that of an unconscious being.*

Some people have reported having near-death experiences. Almost all of those who have reported having such an experience have said that it was an emotionally fulfilling state of being. This tells me that even when our survival is threatened, that it is possible for us to fulfill our purpose. My observation is that these people were not, in fact, having a near-death experience but instead were having a life experience. Many people who have rigid beliefs seem to occasionally have near-life experiences. They have moments of joy and peace intermittently dispersed throughout their lives. Usually, I have found that they have a fundamental belief that says life is difficult and a struggle. Therefore, they believe that they should struggle throughout life—and they do.

We introduce much melodrama into our lives just to support the belief that we can't live a perfect life. If our lives become too *perfect*, we will even seek out drama in the form of entertainment. By becoming emotionally involved with dramatic entertainment, we start to align with the feelings and the beliefs that support that same drama in our own lives.

This means that we become convinced that a "normal" life consists of stress, problems, and difficulties. In our desire to be normal, we seek out friends, family, and even strangers with whom we can share our problems and stories. We believe that if we find someone with a more sensational story to tell, our lives are not that bad. I believe this is why we have an insatiable appetite for talk shows, news broadcasts, movies, plays, and books that sensationalize the abnormal. Unfortunately, as we begin to be influenced by this type of mental input, we also subconsciously sensationalize our own lives. Have you ever noticed how people start to support others in their drama? We normally call this gossip, and the discussion is often around why someone's life is not perfect. While we relate to and are drawn into the stories, we usually cease to stay focused on fulfilling our own purpose.

When I consult with individuals, they typically want to give me all the details about who is involved and what has happened in their lives. I have discovered that this information is typically unimportant and irrelevant to the beliefs that will ultimately allow the person to fulfill his or her purpose. What I have also found is that when people want to tell me about their drama, they usually do not know their purpose and they don't focus on what they want. As a result, they often perceive that their problems are someone else's fault or that they are at the mercy of some circumstance outside of their influence.

This kind of victim mentality keeps many people feeling helpless and vulnerable. When we feel vulnerable, we have a tendency to want to strike out or withdraw from others as a form of protection. Similar behavior can be seen with cats, dogs, and other animals when they are suspicious and fearful.

Your Strengths and Weaknesses

Behold that which is held in creativity.

When we view ourselves as victims, we may feel abused, disrespected, unappreciated, or taken advantage of. As victims, we usually feel a sense of helplessness or weakness. But we can respond to life circumstances with emotional fulfillment and success, without dwelling on our weakness.

Too often, I hear people speak about their strengths and weaknesses. One of the most frequently asked questions during job interviews is, "What are your strengths and weaknesses?" I suppose that someone cleverly came up with the idea to stump job applicants during their interviews to see how they would react. As interviewees contemplate their weaknesses, they no longer support their purpose. I have never met anyone who felt good about his or her perceived shortcomings. How does believing that we have weaknesses support our purpose? It seems that there is little benefit to have others admit to their weaknesses. People who ask others to imagine themselves as weak do them a disservice. When we allow ourselves to be diminished by finding evidence that suggests we are not perfectly capable, we also undermine our purpose. Unfortunately, in some cultures we are expected to be humble, and anyone who is too self-confident is labeled "arrogant."

The concept that we are not whole or fully capable has kept many people feeling incomplete. The belief that we have weaknesses undermines our focus on our ability to create the *essence* of what we want. Any time we acknowledge our weaknesses, we are not honoring our true power. When I meet people, I seldom see them as weak, unhealthy, and unhappy beings although I might see them as being unclear about their purpose and unaware of their beliefs. Once we recognize and believe in the power of our imagination, we can also begin to more fully see possibilities for living our *essence*.

Many people consciously and subconsciously choose partners who they believe will balance their perceived personality weaknesses. We often hear the cliché, "Opposites attract." If we choose this belief, we will select partners who we believe are our opposite. Once we are with our opposite, it is difficult to see how we are similar. This concept of honoring each other's diversity undermines our ability to create harmony and effective communication in our relationships. The reason is simple: We communicate best with those who we feel we can relate to and trust. The belief that people are inherently different causes us to focus on the differences and not the commonality. Focusing on our differences is a distraction from acknowledging our shared purpose. Do you believe you will have more satisfying relationships with people that you have much in common with or with those who you perceive as different? The belief that others are different than ourselves does not support our feeling connected in our relationships.

The belief that we each have weaknesses does not support us in building strong relationships. If we want to have truly happy relationships, we must be truly happy people. I have never met an unhappy person who had a happy relationship. I have never met an angry person who lived a peaceful life. I have never met a spiteful person who lived a life of love. I have never met a dishonest person who was trusting. I have never met a weak person who has strong relationships. Have you?

Realizing Your Own "Victimstance"

We have all been victims of life, love,
and the pursuit of happiness.
Now what?

Humans who believe they are victims want to be rescued and find themselves becoming dependent on others for their well-being. This phenomenon can be observed in personal relationships or even in the relationships we have with our employer or the government. If we believe that others are to blame for our unhappiness, then, in turn, we may also believe that they are also responsible for our happiness.

In our fear of staying unhappy, we do not trust and thus become manipulative. We begin to adopt a scarcity consciousness and believe we need to take advantage of others before they take advantage of us. This type of "me versus them" perspective sets up a situation where one person must lose for the other to win. From our *essence*, most of us want to make a contribution to the lives of others. The win/lose scenario contradicts the premise of adding value to others' lives. For instance, if we see ourselves as winners, then someone else must be the loser. How can we make a contribution to others if we don't already see them as perfect and capable? By contrast, if we see ourselves as losers, we fail to recognize our power to make a contribution to others.

Some people consciously and also unconsciously have learned subtle ways to use their victimstance to manipulate others. They may use their victimstance as a way to induce guilt in others, knowing that the guilty person will be more vulnerable. I have also heard people admit to their short-comings, weaknesses, faults, and problems just so they can gain compassion and sympathy from others. They believe that if they create the image that they are in the process of healing or growing, then their behavior can be excused. The unsuspecting victim of this kind of manipulative tactic will normally not confront or challenge the manipulator. The victim of this manipulation believes that the behavior will soon vanish. This is when the deceit becomes effective.

If the truth be told, someone who is personally aware will take the responsibility to modify his or her beliefs, emotions, and behavior to support the fulfillment of his or her purpose. People who claim to be in process (who are *"trying," "working on," "going through," and "healing"*) probably do not know or are not focused on and committed to their purpose. These people often lack integrity for their loving intention. That is why sometimes we see people whose behavior doesn't seem to align with the message they verbally deliver. This form of lie or deceit simply means they don't believe that what they are telling you is true.

We can only fulfill our purpose when we are fulfilling our purpose. *Trying* to fulfill our purpose is not the same as living with purpose. We can only be healthy when we believe we are healthy. We can only be happy when we believe we are happy. I received a long-distance call from someone who was seeking clarity in her life. I asked, "Is the sun shining where you are?" The woman replied, "No, it's cloudy here." I then said, "It must be very dark where you are if the sun is not shining." She responded, "Well, the sun is shining above the clouds." "Precisely," I said. How we experience life depends on how we approach happiness. If we are trying to be happy, we may not feel as satisfied as we would feel if we simply acknowledged our happiness. In other words, we are only aware that the sun is shining when we choose to believe it is.

I often have people explain to me that they are trying or wanting to be in good relationships, or they want to be writers, actors, teachers, facilitators, doctors, lawyers, good parents, and so forth. I tell each of them that as long as they don't acknowledge that they are already successful communicators, entertainers, educators, facilitators, healers, mediators, nurturers, or spouses, that they have just missed the opportunity to be successful. The path to success is believing that we are actually creating what we want in every moment. People don't succeed by talking about what they are *trying* to create. They succeed by keeping the vision clear and knowing that their vision is constantly unfolding in a way that is consistent with their purpose. Once again, it is the belief system that determines how successful we are at fulfilling our purpose. Seeing ourselves or others as victims undermines our ability to create joy in our lives.

Many of us don't realize that the beliefs we learn from others may not apply to our own lives. In fact, adopting someone else's belief without determining if that belief supports our purpose can actually undermine our success. Even our own beliefs about our experiences or memories influence our current reality. Often we carry with us beliefs that are outdated or that are no longer relevant to our present circumstance. Some people refer to these as "old beliefs," when, in fact, they are current beliefs that do not serve our purpose. What we sometimes call "old baggage" is not really "old." These are merely beliefs that were instilled previously and that remain active in our imagination. With every passing moment and thought, we select beliefs that we choose to apply to our past, present, and future. In this sense, we only have "new baggage" or beliefs that either support or undermine our purpose.

The woman whose purpose is to establish loving, harmonious relationships does not benefit from the belief that men are jerks. While her former husband or boyfriend may well have been inconsiderate, the belief is now outdated and does not support her in establishing loving relationships with men. However, as long as she believes all men are jerks, she will continue to find evidence—in her relations with men—that supports that belief. To move beyond this restrictive belief, she will need to make a responsible choice to engage a belief that allows her to see men as loving, communicative, sensitive, and considerate. As the evidence mounts to support this new belief, she will start to attract men who support her purpose. The benefit, of course, is that she now has the opportunity to have exactly what she wants, instead of perpetuating what she doesn't want.

I was speaking with a man who was having difficulty maintaining relationships in his life. He found himself constantly job-hopping and unable to participate lovingly in an intimate relationship with his girlfriend. I asked him what was the cause of his difficulties, and he said that he was a recovering alcoholic. When I asked him when he would be recovered, he said, "Never." Guess what? Despite the fact that he had stopped drinking, he saw himself as an incurable alcoholic and he continued the behavior that he believed to be that of an alcoholic, which was unreliable, argumentative, uncooperative, and so forth. His belief kept him re-affirming that he was not a healthy and honorable person.

While twelve-step programs have assisted many people to improve their lives, such programs may also be keeping some from fulfilling their purpose. The recovery theme, combined with the belief that they are diseased, imperfect, or flawed in some way, obstructs their vision to see their true purpose and keeps them attached to the support group. Those who shift their dependence and addiction from a substance to the support group—and keep it there—may miss the opportunity to become self-reliant and to make responsible life choices that help them fulfill their purpose.

Some people maintain themselves as victims of their inner child. Whenever they find themselves in emotionally hurtful situations, they can easily use the wounded child as an excuse for their hurt feelings. They may have a belief that their inner child is still wounded or will never grow up. Guess what? The adults who believe that they have a wounded inner child will continue to feel slighted, unappreciated, devalued, disrespected, and victimized. The belief that they possess the spirit of a wounded child does not support them to fulfill their purpose and to sustain feelings of joy, peace, and love. Why not choose to believe that we are strong, healthy, capable adults and children instead?

Your Health or Your Belief

Sickness is the time
when we learn how to be healthy.

By not recognizing our wellness we become victims of the belief that we are weak or ill. As a result of this belief, we diminish our trust in our own immune system to combat even the common cold. This may explain why many people are quick to use drugs instead of allowing their body to naturally heal itself. The more we become dependent on over-the-counter or prescription drugs, the less our natural immunities are used, and we become less resistant to illness. Believing that we are diseased or not well does not support our purpose.

Most of us don't feel very energetic or fulfilled when we believe we are sick. As long as we believe that we have the ability to fulfill our purpose, we can see ourselves as healthy. Again, this does not imply that we should never seek assistance from the medical community. It means we need to be aware of our bodies and our states of mind. When we focus on our physical well-being as the primary indicator of our health, we tend to ignore the powerful significance of our spiritual and emotional health. Have you ever wondered how some of those who are labeled as disabled still live with joy? It is because they don't believe the so-called "disability" is a hindrance to creating the *essence* of what they want emotionally. If we believe seeing a doctor will assist us in fulfilling our purpose, then we will make the responsible decision.

In one instance, a woman believed she was suffering from chronic fatigue syndrome. When I asked her how she knew she had the disease, she said she was unable to participate in the number of physically demanding activities that she once did. Further exploration revealed that her true reasons for not participating were not purely related to her health. In this case, she had used other circumstances as evidence to support her belief that she was not well. It was also interesting that the onset of her disorder coincided with some very traumatic incidents many years earlier. In speaking with this person, it was clear that she harbored much anger and resentment. Like the gentleman who was diagnosed as being terminally ill with cancer, this woman also believed only what she had been told by her doctor and proceeded to manufacture evidence to prove the doctor right.

In both cases, the doctors most likely gave an accurate diagnosis. Yet there was little consideration given to the beliefs that led up to the manifestation of the diseases or the beliefs, still in place, that related to illness instead of wellness. These individuals became victims of their own beliefs about their past, present, and future health. When we focus our attention on the pathology of our being, we see illness; likewise, when we focus on wellness, we see healthy beings.

Many people believe overcoming challenges, growing, and being in process are what makes life worthwhile. While we continue to grow and expand, we often do not reap the emotional benefits of our efforts. Creating new conflicts and adversity in our lives seldom brings us joy and contentment. Every time we introduce a belief that we have been mistreated, we undermine our ability to make a significant contribution to our own purpose and to the emotional well-being of those whose lives we touch, especially the lives of our children.

Chapter 12

Becoming the Wizard in Your Life

*The only expert who can fulfill your purpose
is you.*

We must become the experts in our own lives. Those who we see as experts are those who we recognize as masters of a particular subject matter or set of beliefs. Their beliefs may support us in fulfilling our purpose, or they may not. I find it ironic when I hear two experts who don't agree. I might conclude that possibly neither of them is an expert or perhaps they are merely experts regarding their own beliefs.

Scientists, futurists, strategists, planners, psychics, and astrologers are experts at choosing beliefs that can be proven in the physical realm. In some instances, they are accurate with their predictions, and in other cases, we may not see the manifestation of their predictions. If we choose to adopt the belief of a so-called expert, we increase the chances of experiencing *their* predictions and not our own. When we become experts in our own lives, other people's predictions have little value. To create accurate predictions in our own lives, we must identify our purpose and commit to that purpose in every moment.

To be the expert in your life you will want to listen carefully to everything you say and how you say it. You may want to write down the statements you make to yourself and others and then review them to see if your inventory of beliefs are supporting you in creating what you want. You will probably discover that you have many beliefs that conflict or undermine your creation of the success you want. After you write down your beliefs, you may review them and ask yourself the following question: "How does this belief help me feel happy, joyful, relaxed, calm, peaceful, loving, energetic, enthusiastic, fulfilled, harmonious, connected, whole, complete, strong, or any other word that describes my purpose?" If you find that a belief does not assist you in your purpose, then you have the responsibility to discard that belief. If you do not consciously decide to discard the belief, you will live out of integrity with your purpose. The consequence for living out of integrity is to live feeling unhappy, dissatisfied, stressed, frustrated, anxious, irritated, angry, victimized, empty, lonely, depressed, weak, separated, and struggling, to name a few states of being.

Many people, I have discovered, don't realize that almost every time we have a thought it reflects a belief that we have. Almost everything we say is based on a belief. Listen to the next thought you have or to the next words that you speak. What is the belief that corresponds to that thought or statement? Perhaps the thought or statement itself is a belief.

What we soon realize is that our entire lives are experienced through our beliefs. This is overwhelming for some people because they have a belief (fear) that to make changes in a belief system requires a lot of work. They may say to themselves, "I can't dismantle everything I've been taught to believe since childhood." That is itself a belief that may not be supportive of their purpose. I believe that much of what we believe has value in our lives. So the good news is we don't have to change all of our beliefs; we simply have to dispose of the beliefs that don't bring us the emotional responses that we want. That is why we have emotions. They help to alert us to the fact that our beliefs are either in alignment with our purpose or that we need a change of belief or a "belief realignment" in order to experience the emotions we really want.

If you are one of those people who says, "I'm not sure this will actually work," then chances are it won't. It won't actually work if you try to analyze the validity of this approach from a purely philosophical point of view. To experience the benefits of this approach you must actually begin to explore and discard beliefs in your life that do not bring you joy and contentment. To fulfill your purpose you must consciously choose to create what you want. If you avoid applying your creativity, you may not trust yourself to create what you want in all aspects of your life. In this circumstance, you may believe you are safer letting fate determine your experiences. This belief undermines your ability to fulfill your purpose and to share lovingly with others. Now is the time to create exactly what you want in your life.

Superstition is another form of belief. When I played basketball in college, I was superstitious. Many athletes, I noticed, had rituals or traditions that they believed would make them more successful. Whether or not I made or missed a basket, I would still hold on to the belief that I would shoot more accurately if I bounced the ball three times before shooting a free throw. I also had beliefs about how to wear my hair, socks, and sweat bands. In hindsight, I now realize that all of these beliefs were merely distractions. I am certain I would have been more fulfilled had I been focusing on having fun instead of on my hair and socks.

When we attach significant meaning to our superstitions, we become closed-minded. We become rigid in our beliefs, and life then becomes more challenging (instead of easier) as we resist circumstances that upset our ritual or routine. Many people harbor superstitions because they want a sense of structure in their lives. Often, the need for structure in our lives comes from fear. We believe structure gives us security. But what exactly is "security"? I have discovered that security is just an illusion based on the belief that life will not change for the worse. A sense of security helps us to feel safe, when, in fact, we may not be.

For instance, many people stay in relationships or jobs that are not satisfying because the routine appears to give them security. They may sacrifice fulfilling their true desires to start their own business because they feel more secure working for a large company. The size of the company, of course, may have little to do with how successful it is. Since large companies are not necessarily safe havens, those people who focus on security or safety are probably not directing their attention to what they would prefer to create in their lives.

I spent sixteen years as an employee for several large companies. While that experience was extremely rewarding and valuable, I often felt stifled. However, my position was financially lucrative and I enjoyed the benefits of international travel and prestige. I believed that I had security. Yet my purpose was not being fulfilled. By letting go of my beliefs about security, I was able to create a lifestyle that is far more fulfilling. I am not just working for a paycheck or security anymore. I now have a sense of freedom, creativity, accomplishment, contribution, and joy. I am fulfilling my purpose.

When we are fulfilling our purpose we are less dependent on the need for structure. Often, structure impedes our sense of freedom and undermines our purpose. When we become less spontaneous, for example, we might miss opportunities to create new experiences that allow us to feel light, free, and energized. By giving up our spontaneity, we also lose much of our childlike qualities. As adults, we are often not sure how to integrate playfulness and a sense of responsibility. We can regain our sense of wonderment by knowing our purpose and not being afraid to live with integrity.

Many of us live outside the bounds of our integrity and in a state of adult theatrics. This means we subscribe to an image that we believe makes others see us as mature. However, maturity is not an image but a state of being. If we want to be seen as mature, responsible, and powerful, we must not allow others to keep us from fulfilling our purpose. When we live in alignment with our *essence*, we project a very stable, centered, and powerful image. Some will test us to see if we are authentic in our purpose. If we stay firm in our commitment, others will acknowledge our expertise and leadership and support us. Being an expert in our own lives is essential if we are to fulfill our purpose.

Follow the Leader

Effective leaders listen to themselves and discover the beliefs that fulfill their purpose.

Leadership is often thought to be the ability to direct, influence, and command people. True leadership is not about other people. True leaders are not self-appointed nor are they appointed by a group. Think about the people you know who you consider to be effective leaders. Are these people who have only goals, or do they have a purpose?

Having goals with no purpose leads to a feeling of emptiness even after we achieve our goals. These people may not be famous, but they have a mission to fulfill their purpose. We become leaders when we realize and live according to our *essence* and purpose. The only way we can be effective leaders is by believing that we can lead ourselves and fulfill our own purpose.

Self-leadership is a by-product of personal responsibility and clarity of purpose. Many think that we exercise self-leadership when we set and achieve goals for ourselves. Perhaps we believe that our goals are the passport to personal success and happiness. We have a tendency to view others as leaders and role models instead of assuming our role as a self-authority. Because we each have a unique set of beliefs that we live by, no one else can actually tell us how to attain our goals or fulfill our purpose. Like I am doing, they can only tell you how they believe they accomplish their own success.

Sometimes when people achieve their goals, they get a brief emotional high along with their sense of accomplishment. Shortly thereafter, they may feel empty and feel the need to set another goal to get that same high feeling. In a sense, the process of setting goals and attaining them becomes like a drug that people take in order to get the emotional high. Without this goal-oriented process, some people feel their life experiences have less value. However, if the purpose of attaining goals is to feel emotionally fulfilled, why must they wait until they reach their goals?

Self-leadership is about finding the beliefs that allow us to fulfill our purpose regardless of what goals we set or reach. The emotional rewards that we expect from our goals are available to us at any time. Often when we set goals we assume that we don't already have what we want. The intention of achieving a goal is to provide the physical evidence that we can have what we want. The emotional high wears off as we begin to realize that the physical manifestation of our goals alone does not sustain our purpose.

Those who do not know their purpose are more likely to look to others for leadership. As followers, we ignore our own purpose and subscribe to the belief that joy comes from our being accepted by others. This kind of superficial acceptance is not based on the beauty of our own magnificence. We find ourselves trapped by our need for constant attention and validation. We believe that we need attention from others to reassure our level of acceptance by those whose opinions we value. **Believe it or not, there is no greater opinion than the one we hold of ourselves.**

View from the Mountaintop

Heaven exists for those whose beliefs
bring peace and joy to the soul.

People often describe their personal growth experience as a never-ending journey. Along their journey, they experience and overcome challenges that are followed by moments of personal revelation and insight. One such insight might be that the true challenge and opportunity in our lives is for us to bring the awareness about our beliefs to consciousness. Once we live consciously with purpose, we begin to realize the beauty, wonder, and magnificence of our existence.

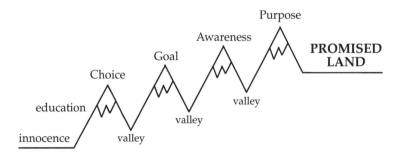

In keeping with the theme of a journey, I have created the previous illustration that represents a common journey through life. As we are born into this world, we enter with innocence. Our beliefs about the world have not yet been established. Through numerous vehicles of social programming, such as parents, schools, churches, clubs, gangs, teams, government, and other organizations, we begin to amass a set of beliefs about our lives. Often we refer to these beliefs as knowledge. As we ascend the first mountain in search of knowledge, we see the many choices that are available to us. At the crest of Choice Mountain we can see in many directions. From this vantage point, we can decide where we might want to travel to next.

With knowledge and the opportunity to make choices in our lives, we usually set goals for ourselves. These goals often involve lifestyle choices regarding relationships, careers, material possessions, and related aspirations. We continue our journey on the way to achieving our goals. As we progress, we enter valleys where we must gain additional knowledge about the goal we are trying to reach. Some may lose sight of their goal or become discouraged while in the valleys. Those who reach the top of Goal Mountain realize that with knowledge and experience, they are more self-aware and confident.

Of course, why would anyone stay on Goal Mountain if they were self-aware? So we believe we deserve to be on the top of Awareness Mountain. Again, we must follow a similar path, as we continue our journey to the top of Awareness. The valley between Goal and Awareness Mountains is filled with challenges and fears that we must overcome. Those who stay focused on achieving personal awareness may reach the top of Awareness Mountain. With knowledge, experience, and awareness, we realize that we truly have a purpose in this life.

Those with determination decide to discover their purpose, and they set forth on a journey to conquer Purpose

Mountain. This often seems to be the most difficult part of our life journey. However, those who manage to ascend Purpose Mountain are rewarded with a view of the Promised Land. The Promised Land is where people who honor their integrity live. These people have rearranged their lives and beliefs in order to support the *essence* of what they want. They live every day with bliss, grace, gratitude, and purpose.

Examine the illustration on page 119 and mark a spot anywhere along the path which describes where you believe you are on your life journey. Are you ascending one of the mountains? Are you descending one of the mountains? Are you in a valley or on the top of one of these mountains? Have you reached the top of Purpose Mountain or the Promised Land?

After you make your mark, ask yourself why you believe you are where you are. If you did not mark that you are at least on top of Purpose Mountain, you are not integrating your knowledge, experience, awareness, or purpose to your benefit. You still have a belief that keeps you from fulfilling your purpose. It is probably the belief that you are not living your *essence*.

How you see it is that you are not yet fulfilling your purpose. *How you don't see it* is that you may not be on a journey anymore since you already know your purpose. Once you know your purpose, the only way you can be at the top of Purpose Mountain is by believing that you are at the top of the mountain fulfilling your purpose.

Next time you have a thought, I trust that you will discover the magic and power of selecting only those beliefs that allow you to *realize* that you are already living in the Promised Land.

*Somewhere in your life a miracle
waits patiently for your next belief!*

AFTERWARDS

I trust that you will use this book as a resource to help you realize that your quest for personal awareness serves no useful purpose unless you are prepared to use it to create the *essence* of what you want in your life. This means you must be willing to integrate your awareness about your beliefs and let that awareness assist you to build the life experience that you want.

You can always compare yourself to others and find evidence to support why you can't live to your heart's desire. Perhaps you believe it is easier for others because their circumstances are not like yours. You also have the option to accept your role as the expert in your life and take the initiative to fulfill your purpose with joyful results. You may begin by letting go of the belief that your life will be or has to be difficult. When you assume your position as the wizard in your life, you can invent magic. You don't have to wait for someone else to show you how to make your life better or perfect. However, if you expect or want someone to tell you how to live your life, there are many people who will assume that responsibility for you. Those people may not be clear on their own purpose and may have their own agenda ahead of yours, in which case you will take advice and listen to a multitude of opinions without the benefit of feeling fulfilled, content, satisfied, and happy.

People who have read this book have told me that they feel relaxed, calm, hopeful, empowered, joyful, and optimistic. Any time that we acknowledge possibilities in our lives we feel enriched. If you experience some of these same emotions, I suspect it is because you are allowing your beliefs to see new opportunities for personal freedom that are not disguised by circumstantial evidence. The true rewards in life come when we consistently apply those beliefs that help us focus only on our own purpose, and help us avoid worrying about how others are living their lives.

I believe that you can commit to your purpose and allow the beauty and miracle of your life to unfold with trust, awareness, and knowledge. Just believe you can!

Forever is never ever far away

ABOUT THE AUTHOR

David B. Bolen, II, is the author of *The Essence of Living: Reaching Beyond Global Insanity*. He is also the founder of Shared Knowledge, a company which aids those who seek personal awareness and empowerment through seminars, workshops, and private sessions. Prior to committing to his purpose in life, he worked for sixteen years in several large corporations as an international marketing strategist, planner, and consultant. As the son of a diplomat and ambassador, he grew up on three continents and has traveled extensively since his youth. He has shared his philosophy with people worldwide and finds that at the *essence* of our being we each aspire to a common human experience. His books are inspired from his own life awareness and experience. He has a bachelor's degree from the University of Colorado, and he proclaims a standing of L.C.H.B. (Licensed and Certified Human Being).